A Prince Too Far

A Prince Too Far
The Great Powers and the Shaping of Modern Albania

Ferdinando Salleo
Translated from the Italian
by Roland Flamini

Washington, DC

Copyright © 2015 by Ferdinando Salleo
The photographs © Enzo Sellerio Editore.

New Academia Publishing, 2016
Italian edition, *Albania, un regno per sei mesi*, © 2000 Enzo Sellerio Editore

All rights reserved. No part of this book may be reproduced or transmitted in any form or by any means, electronic or mechanical, including photocopying, recording, or by any information storage and retrieval system.

Printed in the United States of America

Library of Congress Control Number: 2015955750
ISBN 978-0-9966484-2-4 paperback (alk. paper)

 An imprint of New Academia Publishing

 New Academia Publishing, LLC
4401-A Connecticut Ave., NW #236, Washington DC 20008
www.newacademia.com - info@newacademia.com

For Anne Marie

*Those who cannot remember the past
are condemned to repeat it*
(George Santayana, *The Life of Reason*, 1905)

Contents

Prelude to the Great War	1
Albania's National Awakening and Autonomy	7
The Balkan Wars and Albanian Independence	15
Albania and the Great Powers	21
The Reign of the Prince of Wied	27
"The Events at Durazzo"	45
A War Begins: A Short-lived Reign Ends	63
Italian and Austro-Hungarian Diplomacy in Albania	73
Conclusions	87
Notes	95
Bibliography	97
Glossary	98
Photo Gallery	101

Prelude to the Great War

In the years preceding the two great conflicts of the Twentieth Century Europe was on the brink of war more than once, pushed there by the expansionist ambitions of the great Powers, their industrial, naval, and military interests, the surge of nationalism, the obsessive fear of encirclement and the temptation of pre-emptive war. Each crisis was averted through the caution of seasoned, realist statesmen, and the reluctance of large sections of the public, often the majority, to let itself be led by hot headed minorities. In the end, political and diplomatic negotiation managed to resolve the crisis in a flurry of exchanged notes, drum rolls, secret agreements and public statements, the complex mechanisms of unwritten understandings. The compromise held until the next crisis.

If there was no war, neither was there peace. Each successive crisis left residual traces in the public memory, sharpened by emotional and often sensational media coverage (the CNN factor in an earlier form), and by internal political factors. Such memories were cumulative, with the compromises becoming more intolerable to public opinion than the conflicts they had averted. People were increasingly mesmerized by the notion that war was inevitable but could be limited, and would re-confirm the principles and ambitions that had from time to time been invoked to justify political and diplomatic action. The progressive and irreversible weakening of the Ottoman Empire had intensified the rivalry among the Powers—as the main protagonists of the politics of Europe were fearfully referred to—over the Balkans, strategically positioned with access to the Mediterranean and the Black Sea, the Europe of the Danube, and the South-East. The dangerous instability of the Balkans directly involved Europe in a turbulent area divided by frontiers that were often in dispute, riddled with revisionism, and tormented by conspiracies and conflicts.

The Albanians found themselves suddenly free from Ottoman domination just as the rest of Europe trembled on the edge of the great European conflagration. A patchwork of clans, different religions and ethnic groups occupied real estate that the Powers had designated a sovereign principality and entrusted to a German prince, Wilhelm of Wied. The Albanian factor fitted awkwardly into Balkan politics, and the reasons were many. They ranged from the backwardness of the population to their adherence to ancestral customs, to their continued ties with Constantinople, to the tribal structure of their society, to their religious and ethnic differences, and finally the rivalry with areas that had once formed part of the Albanian nation. Independent Albania emerged in this climate.

The presence of military and naval forces from the European Powers, the delicate regional balance, and the prickly relations among the Prince of Wied's European advisers, like the rivalry and the antics of the various Albanian tribal leaders, has for us an uncanny topical flavor, recalling events in the major newspapers and the television news from the same region of Europe, the Balkans, so close yet so foreign.

The postcards (actually news photographs) sent by the Marquis of San Giuliano, minister of foreign affairs for the kingdom of Italy, to his daughter-in-law during those anxious months between April and September 1914 show us the Albania which the Prince of Wied was expected by the Powers to transform from a former Turkish province into a "vital and progressive" European state. The images are a vivid record of the dramatic events of the prince's six-month reign, the insurrections, betrayals, the outbreak of the European war, and the consequent decline of interest in the little Balkan principality in the Adriatic, the end of the reign as Albania sank back into the morass of tribes, clans, beys and armed gangs.

The Balkan war had re-drawn the peninsula at great human cost. Nationalism had been victorious on the edge of Europe. The war had destroyed "Turkish Europe," replacing it with a Slavic threat to Austria-Hungary that was causing concern in Vienna. Italy and Austria-Hungary faced off in the region, but had to set aside their rivalry to collaborate in Durrës, the Prince's capital, each with the intention of giving life to an Albania that would not be within the other nation's sphere of influence, but would be "vital and progressive." Despite this common purpose an atmosphere of mutual suspicion and hostility prevailed between Rome and Vienna, the result of Italian irredentism and Austrian myopia, complicated by the Slavic factor, and Hungarian *hubris*.

Minister of Foreign Affairs Antonino Paternò Castello, Marquis of San Giuliano.

4 A Prince Too Far

The growing instability in Europe and the storm that was scudding down on the whole continent, made the Albanian situation even more complex forcing the Powers—particularly Austria-Hungary and Italy, whose strategy was already very difficult—to be engaged in a continuous exercise of diplomatic and political fine tuning that tried the patience of government ministers towards their representatives in Albania. Despite the disputes, the open antagonism, the intrigues against each other and against the Prince of Wied, the often dubious loyalty of the officials in country and the intelligence agents, Rome and Vienna tried to the very end to preserve the agreed plan for Albania, preferably without undermining their own separate long term intentions.

Looking at the events of those six months now, with the horrors of the more recent Balkan conflict still fresh in the memory, becomes cinematic: a difficult exercise in flashbacks and flash forward. The photographs sent by San Giuliano to his daughter-in-law, the dispatches and editorials in the newspapers of the time, the diplomatic documents review-

Reverse of postcard sent by the Marquis of San Giuliano to his daughter-in-law.

ing progress or sending instructions to ambassadors, resurrect a distant and unreal world, rendered more remote by the grand period uniforms, the Turkish-style fezzes worn by the Albanians, the bearded dignitaries, the *redingotes* and *turqueries*, the horses, adventurers, and women. Also, sadly, the batteries of artillery, the piles of corpses lying in shallow graves, the lines of refugees, the guerrillas and the troops in battle formation, public opinion inflamed by demagogic speeches, the reassuring international conferences. But is it so remote after all? Much of it seems recognizable from what we have seen and read in the past few years, in our time, without the fancy uniforms and the Oriental costumes that make the Prince and the pashas distant figures.

Maria Paterno' Castello, Marchioness of Capizzi, to whom the postcards were addressed.

Historians explain the political objectives behind the Powers' decision to invent a European state where there had been no European state, to create a police force and a judicial system, a parliament, and even the glimmerings of a foreign policy. A remarkable multi-national collaborative effort–more geopolitics than benevolence, but nonetheless a huge undertaking–was directed at bringing stability and a viable public structure to the principality: which is another link with the present day.

trian slip-up, such as its support for the creation of a Uniate community in Elbasan, which infuriated the Orthodox hierarchy. But the Austrians took their relationship with the Catholics seriously, lavished money on the project, and–it was said–had the support of the Vatican. The Italians took a secular approach in their schools, sidestepping the religious differences in Albania, thus leaving that area to the Austrians. Only the Franciscan friars of Shkoder were Italian. In the Shkoder *vilayet* the Orthodox gravitated towards the Italians for support because Vienna backed the Catholics.

This conditioned the Austrian strategy, as well as the Italian insistence on always keeping in sight the Muslim majority, and Rome's warning to the Prince to be cautious in favoring the Catholic mountain tribes of the Mirdites and the Malissori in view of their growing animosity towards the Muslims.

In 1903, Antonino di San Giuliano, who was to become a key protagonist in the "six-month reign," published in the *Giornale d'Italia* a series of reports on his voyage in the Balkans, entitled *Lettera sull'Albania*. The Catania-born statesman, a good and careful writer who had published a study of contemporary socio economic conditions in Sicily, had been minister for posts in the Pelloux cabinet, and was soon to become foreign minister for the first time, a post he held again during the Albanian crisis until his death on October 16, 1914. His description of society under Ottoman rule and of popular aspirations–at least, as expressed by members of the upper class whom he met–helped form the political and strategic thinking that we later see reflected in his diplomacy.

He saw Albania as a pivotal state in the Adriatic, its strategic position of value to both Italy and Austria-Hungary.

The geopolitics and geo-economics of the Balkan Peninsula had been a factor in Italian political thinking for some time. The area was considered with as much attention and care as the Mediterranean. In May of 1904, Tittoni, declared that, "whoever held the narrowest point in the Adriatic can control access in and out of that sea. The position, like that of the entire coast of Albania, would make a natural entrance to a large part of the western Balkans, where the topography of the land allows it." San Giuliano anticipated a major trans-Balkan infrastructure when he talked about "the construction of a railroad along the Adriatic coastline to the Vardar valley through southern Albania."

The physical characteristics of the country determined the pace and manner in which this ancient people had evolved. Mountain chains running north-south encouraged communication in that same direction, but made lateral, cross-country movement virtually impossible. Over the years, the differences in appearance between mountain and coastal people, and the physical structure of the land began to have an impact on the social and even political development. Throughout Albania the key factor among the land owning class was not a late feudalism, but a network of families and clans governed by unwritten traditions and customs, linked to Ottoman institutions. The society was scattered across a poorly defined area linked by land to the East, and to the West by the Adriatic.

For many centuries right up to the Twentieth Albanians had been firmly integrated into Ottoman culture and society. Religion was one obvious reason; but the other was the role Albanians, including leading personalities, had played in the Sublime Porte. The late blooming nationalism, and the uneven manner in which it developed and spread is reflected in Byron's judgment: *Fierce are Albania's children, yet they lack/ Not virtues, were those virtues more mature.*"[1]

In creating the popular myths that bolster nationalism Albanians could not lay claim to the glories of Greece, the splendors of Byzantium, or of the Slavic kingdoms of the past. So the Skanderbeg cult became the symbol of Albania's new national identity, forgetting that he had fought the Turks as a Christian. In any case, Albanian tribal society had a strong sense of its own culture and its own language, despite classic north-south differences between gheghi (northerners) and toschi (southerners) who speak two separate dialects, but still clearly Albanian. There was also the blood link, as the Prince of Wied discovered to his cost when he tried to use the Albanian troops he had recruited, with officers who had declared their loyalty to him, against the insurgents.

The rise to power of the Young Turks[2] in 1908 signaled a dynamic phase in the emergence of Albania. "Their aggressive, centrist politics awakened Albanian national sentiment," wrote Kemal Bey Vlora, the "father" of Albanian independence. In rejection of the centrist chauvinism of the Young Turks, the Albanians moved in the direction of a separate, national identity. The Albanians edged into independence one stage at a time, and began by seeking the use and teaching of their own language. Several tribal chiefs had different requests which were not necessarily coordinated, but collectively they focused on melding together four *vilayet*[3] into one *pashalik*.

The region was headed by a nominee of the Porte, but administered by Albanian officials enjoying a form of autonomy in which the proceeds of taxes due to the Ottoman Empire were supposed to be re-invested in Albania, around 40 million gold francs per year. San Giuliano noted that "only a minimal amount was spent in Albania."

The Austro-Hungarian–Italian rivalry was an important outside factor in this scenario, which was otherwise fueled by reasons far removed from the Nineteenth Century romantic movements that had produced in Europe an interest in the Hellenic nation, still strong in England and Germany. That rivalry between Vienna and Rome led to a mutual support for the emergence of a sovereign, independent Albania; the same rivalry was also a wake-up call for Albanian nationalism.

Early in 1910, the internal situation in Albania and the country's relations with the Porte slid into serious deterioration when an uprising broke out in Kosovo, to be quickly repeated by another further south. Fearing that unrest in Albania would spread to other parts of the empire and undermine the Young Turks' political program of rebirth, the government decided to use force, particularly in Kosovo. The Kosovars had emerged as the front line of the nascent Albanian nationalist movement, attracting active support from immigrants in Europe and America, as well as from the *arbereshe*, the Albanian communities settled in southern Italy and in Sicily as long ago as the Fifteenth to the Eighteenth

Centuries but still maintaining strong tribal links across the Adriatic.

Constantinople sent Turgut Pasha to the northern *vilayet* with sixteen thousand men, which soon became forty thousand led by the Ottoman minister of war in person.

At first, the strong, well-armed Turkish expedition had the best of it. The Turks accepted Albanian demands (language, administrative autonomy, appointment of Albanian officials in Albania), but they were never put into effect. In March 1911, a revolt of Catholic Malissori north of Shkoder, with support from Montenegrins and Serbs, coincided with widespread unrest in the south. There were violent clashes with Turkish forces, especially in Kosovo, where the uprising had re-surfaced. By mid-May the insurgents were in control of several cities; in June the Catholic Mirdites joined the fray. The Turkish repression intensified. On June 23, 1911, various rebel leaders meeting in Montenegro with Ismail Kemal agreed on a common program in the "Gerche memorandum," a document of great significance in which for the first time a demand for autonomy for all Albania is mentioned as a national objective. In June, Sultan Mehmet V himself was in Kosovo, but even his peace overtures failed to halt the insurrection.

On September 29 Italy declared war on Turkey, and the Porte's situation became more precarious. Turkish setbacks had emboldened the insurgents, and the opening of a second front against Italy further stretched Turkish forces. The Italian action had signaled the end of the status quo whereby the rival political and territorial ambitions of the Great Powers had acted as a mutual deterrent to the advantage of the Ottoman Empire. Now, however, its territorial integrity was no longer beyond challenging. While the war with Italy was going badly for the Turks, the Albanian insurrection gained momentum, spreading from the north across the whole country, increasingly presenting a united political front, overcoming religious and tribal differences. Albanian demands to the Turkish government of Muftar Pasha were the same as before, only now more precisely articulated. The

Albanian central committee memorandum of July 28 again requested autonomy, but always within the empire, and this time defined the area of what later became Albania—most of Kosovo, a province of Serbia, a part of Montenegro, another from Macedonia, and a province from the Greece of today.

On August 2, the Porte renewed some general commitments that no longer satisfied the Albanians. The insurrection intensified, and the rebels continued to advance, resisted with increasing difficulty by the Turkish forces commanded by Ibrahim Pasha, who still occupied Skopje. Large numbers of Turkish troops deserted, and in Constantinople the insurrection served as a catalyst for the officers who opposed the Young Turks. At the end of August 1912, the leaders of the Albanian rebellion gathered in Pristina to dictate to Ibrahim Pasha their terms in fourteen points. In a subsequent meeting in Skopje, Ibrahim accepted their demands, and on September 4 Constantinople confirmed his acceptance. Albanian autonomy had been won, wrested from the Porte at a price. The "contact group" of the day in the shape of the ambassadors of the six Powers that constituted the "European directorate" met in London with Sir Edward Grey, the British foreign secretary as its chairman. On December 20, 1913, the meeting issued a statement saying that, "the ambassadors had recommended in principle, and the governments had accepted, autonomy for Albania." The agreement included a clause giving Serbia commercial access to the Adriatic.

Creating an autonomous country within the Porte had been a cautious answer to a development that had been both sudden and unexpected. If the war of 1913 had not signaled the end of Turkish power in the Balkans, Albania's progression to the next step of independence during that summer would have been very unlikely. The irony of history was that the Balkan wars had pulled the region closer into the complex and dangerous game of the Great Powers.[4]

The Balkan Wars and Albanian Independence

The Albanian insurrection paved the way for the success of Albania's Balkan allies against Turkey, even if at the time the Albanian leaders' role in the Balkan victory failed to win the attention it deserved. Throughout the Italian-Turkish War, the Albanians had forced the Porte into a sequence of alternate stick and carrot tactics. This policy had contributed greatly to the mobilization and organization of Albanian forces and to the emergence of a level of nationalist consciousness that went beyond the traditional pattern of family and clan relationships. It was also a factor in the north-south division of the country, and it sharpened religious differences.

The situation in and around Turkey was very tense, and the Balkan states seized the moment to deal the decisive blow that was to drive the Turks out of Europe. Russia supported the nationalist movement of the Christian states for its own ends, namely to regain its lost influence in the region, and advance its geostrategic interests at the expense of both the

The double-headed eagle emblem of Albania.

Ottoman Empire and Austria-Hungary following its humiliating defeat in the Bosnian crisis.

The first Balkan War left the Turkish army in total disarray from its clash with Italy. At the end of six weeks' fighting the Porte agreed to the London Accord of May 30, 1913, that formalized the end of Turkish Europe. Constantinople surrendered to the four Balkan allies all the territory west of the Enos-Midia Line. Albania's future was entrusted to the European powers.

The Balkan conflict erupted again almost immediately following disputes among the victors over the Turkish spoils. Once again the Balkans were re-shaped, mainly to the advantage of Serbia and Greece. The future of the new state of Albania was cast in doubt even before it had been formally created, but was confirmed as an independent country in the Treaty of Bucharest of August 10, 1913, that ended the second Balkan conflict.

The Balkan allies were involved in a frenetic effort to fulfill their respective territorial ambitions, in the first conflict against the Turks by fomenting revolution among the Catholics in the mountains, arming the guerrillas, attempting to unite rival Albanian leaders. The Serbs even made use of the notorious "Black Hand" terrorist organizations to secure their ends. In the second conflict they quickly moved into Albanian provinces including Kosovo, western Macedonia, Skhoder, and Durrës.

At the start of the Balkan conflict anti-Turkish sentiment ran high among Albanians nationalists involved. But the land grabbing tactics of the Balkan league countries at Albania's expense forced them to side with the Turks, but at the same time continuing to press for their independence. Albanian patriots stressed to the Great Powers that they were fighting alongside the Turks "to defend the territorial integrity and the freedom of Albania." On November 28, 1912, in Valona, they proclaimed their independence after thirty years of effort.

The National Assembly presided over by Ismail Kemal bey Vlora declared independence. A provisional government

Ismail Kemal with Isa Boletini, leader of the Kossovar insurrection against Turkey.

was formed headed by Ismail Kemal, and a senate was created "to control and assist the government" with Essad Pasha Toptani as president. The Albanian flag was raised: the black two-headed eagle of Skanderbeg on a red background, and the Porte and the Great Powers were formally notified.

Albania's autonomy was immediately opposed by Serbia, Montenegro, and Greece, and more so its efforts to unify the four *vilayet*: particularly Kosovo, Monastir, and Ioánina which had mixed populations.

It was in Macedonia that the ethnic upheaval was most violent because it was in that country that the mixture of nationalities was the most chaotic. According to the *Report on the International Commission to inquire into the Causes of the Balkan Wars* published in 1914 by the Carnegie Endowment for International Peace, "the adoption of the Treaty of Bucharest created the strongest moral and social unrest" mainly due to a policy of assimilation conducted with "maniacal vigor." The brutal campaign of arrests, violent treatment, and deportations on ethnic and religious grounds created a nostalgia for Ottoman domination.

Essad Pasha Toptani, president of the Albanian Senate in the transition period before the arrival of the Prince of Wied.

The Balkan Wars and Albanian Independence

The Balkan wars were a biblical scourge in the region. Mass executions of Albanian civilians were carried out by Serbs in the north, more so by the Montenegrins, but most of all in the south by the Greeks. Hatred and religious and racial intolerance led to excesses and destruction throughout most of a country which did not yet exist.

Press accounts and the memoirs of eye-witnesses and others speak of villages razed, mutilations, families destroyed or deported, men and children massacred in a campaign of ethnic cleansing, columns of refugees and collective despair, and every form of violence, foreshadowing in a striking way the reports and images of horrors perpetrated in modern day Bosnia and Kosovo.

The Carnegie report adds its own detailed catalog of testimonials from eye-witnesses of executions and assassinations, fires and drownings, massacres and atrocities, "not only between Muslims and Christians separated by centuries of hatred and religious fanaticism, but also between Bulgarians and Greeks, and between Greeks and Serbs who earlier had joined together in a war of liberation."

Massacre victims in Northern Albania.

The Albania established in London was never fully accepted by its neighbors—by Serbia, Montenegro, Greece. They considered themselves the real victors of the Balkan wars and did not abandon their claim to Albanian territory.

Austria-Hungary and Italy, in close contact, held consultations on November 17, 1913, on delineating Albania's frontiers and its internal organizations, committing themselves jointly to the independence and security of the new state. The Powers accepted the engagement in Rome and Vienna in defending Albanian statehood thereby providing protection against any territorial encroachment of the new state. In that way Europe collectively established its willingness to intervene on Albanian issues.

Balkan stability was a diplomatic priority in the chancelleries of Europe, where the lesson had been learned that hatred among the Balkan states incited local conflicts which, in turn, threatened the general peace by fomenting lack of faith among the Great Powers.

Within this environment Albania achieved statehood as a kind of international protectorate, its full sovereignty inhibited by built-in limitations in the form of multilateral controls that could be made to function with difficulty, and more often did not. This state of affairs grew out of the reality of the internal weakness of the new state and the fact that it existed in a predatory neighborhood.

Albania and the Great Powers

In July 1913, Sir Edward Grey re-convened the Albanian "contact group" to define Albania's independence and bring the new state into existence, with appropriate institutions, organisms and frontiers, and enjoying Europe's full recognition and support. On the 29th the ambassadors' conference determined that Albania should be "constituted as an autonomous, hereditary principality, enjoying full sovereignty guaranteed by the Six Powers who would also nominate its reigning prince."

Turkish suzerainty was specifically ruled out. Albania's neutrality was guaranteed by the Powers. Albania's civil and financial administration was to be entrusted to an international commission made up of one delegate from each of the Powers and an Albanian delegate, all serving for a renewable six-year term. The commission was given six months to prepare an organizational plan for all branches of the new Albanian administration, and to submit to the Powers its conclusions and recommendations.

"The prince shall be nominated within six months. Until the nomination and the formation of a national government the existing local authorities, such as the gendarmerie will be under the jurisdiction of an international committee. An international gendarmerie, commanded by foreign officers, will be responsible for security and public order."

On April 10, 1914, the International Control Commission, meeting in Valona (now Vlore), formally approved the 216 articles of the Albanian Statute, a form of basic law for the newly independent principality. It now remained to give Albania secure and internationally recognized borders–in reality a tall order for a fledgling Balkan state hemmed in by greedy neighbors, in the north Serbia and Montenegro; in the south, Greece. Serbia claimed Kosovo, Macedonia, and an outlet to the sea; Montenegro wanted Scutari (now Shkoder).

The provisional government (as it now was) in Valona had territorial ambitions of its own. The government had its eye on all territory with an Albanian presence, including some areas where it seemed of dubious justification.

Serbia and Montenegro had emerged victorious from the Balkan wars, but can hardly be said to have profited from their success. They were far from resigned to giving up their claim to provinces with mixed Albanian-Serbian populations. Above all, neither state had given its assent to a territorial agreement with the Albanians whom they viewed as not much different from the defeated Turks. The Serbian Prime Minister Nikola Pašić, echoing Bismarck, denied the very existence of "an Albanian nationality."

Italy and Austria-Hungary opposed Serbian and Montenegrin aspirations as well as any that Greece might have. A large Albania, with natural borders was both more viable and an obstacle to Pan-Slavic ambitions. To Austria-Hungary the idea of Serbia with a naval base in the Adriatic was unacceptable. A commercial outlet through Montenegro and Albania was the most that Vienna would tolerate. Russia and France supported Serbia and Greece, so the concept of a vital (read larger) Albania advanced by the Triple Alliance was not embraced in either Paris or Moscow.

In the end, Albania's northern borders were the product of a compromise cobbled together by Sir Edward Grey, and involving some significant concessions. The new state had to be fitted together like a jigsaw puzzle, a piece added here and another subtracted there, Grey told the House of Commons, "in the interests of preserving the agreement between the Powers, and essential to the interests of peace in Europe." Serbs and Greeks were persuaded to pull back from areas which they had annexed, and which were now assigned to Albanian

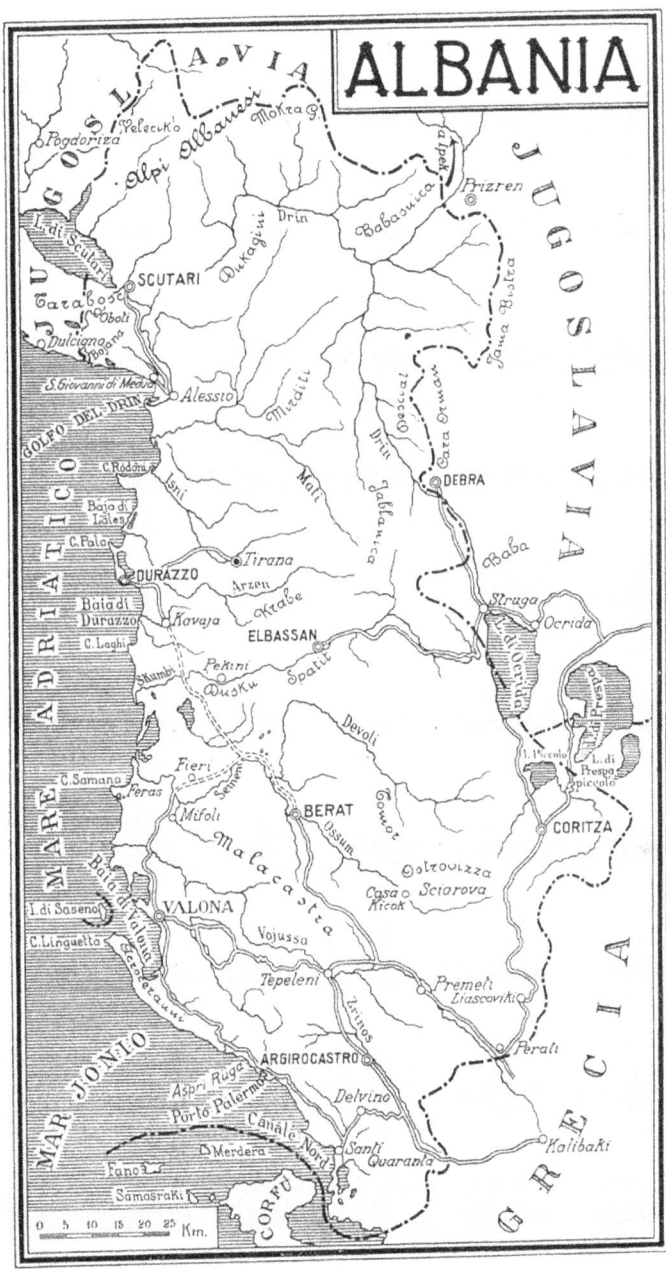

Map of Albania in the 1920s

sovereignty. The Serbs had taken over Medua and Alessio (now Lezhe), and in the south the Greeks had edged into Ioánina and Santi Quaranta (now Saranda). The Austrian foreign minister, Berchtold, gave in to Russian pressure not to include Kosovo and Western Macedonia (including Prizren, Peć—now Peja— and Ochrid) in the new Albania. The Russian minister Sazonov agreed to give up Shkoder to become a major city in the new state. The Albanians in the territories under Serbian or Montenegrin rule were to receive international guarantees of their religious and cultural freedom.

The agreement satisfied the divergent interests of the Powers, but not the Albanians left behind in Serbia and Montenegro. Protest riots followed; and every uprising, every guerrilla attack fueled a Serbian campaign to discredit the new principality as a danger to the stability of the region. The Serbs procrastinated in withdrawing from agreed areas; pressed for fresh border concessions; plotted to create a friendly Albanian government that was not pro-Austrian.

The same with the Montenegrins. It took an international naval blockade and threats from Austria to force the Montenegrins to quit Shkoder. Prime Minister Pašić's commitments to Vienna were more honored in the breach. In the first weeks of October the Serbs began to reoccupy several villages, but were checked by Austrian threats of action. Even so, Pašić said Serbia's withdrawal would depend on what he called "the circumstances in Albania." Austria-Hungary's reaction to the Serbian cat-and-mouse game was a sharply worded ultimatum on October 18. Under no circumstances would Albania's internationally defined borders be changed, and the Serbs had eight days in which to accept them.

France and Russia protested against Vienna's "precipitous action"—while at the same time counseling Belgrade to withdraw. Kaiser Wilhelm II took the opportunity of a visit to Vienna to inveigh against the Slavs. "War between East and West cannot be avoided indefinitely," the Kaiser declared ominously. Meanwhile, the question of Albania's southern borders had been put in the hands of an international commission. Its first meetings were held without the participation of either the Albanians or the Greeks. In March, the latter had helped themselves to Ioánina.

Rome and Vienna extended their naval blockade south to Durrës, warned the Greeks to stay away from Valona, and on December 31 enjoined the government in Athens to withdraw from territories assigned in London to the new Albanian state. The confrontation was resolved by accepting an earlier British proposal submitted in the Florence Protocol of December 19, 1913, whereby Albania got Argirocastro (now Gjirokaster), and Korcia, and Ioánina remained in Greece hands.

Athens tried to link the Greek withdrawal to the Aegean Question, because Italy still had a somewhat tenuous hold on the Dodecanese Islands. But the members of the Triple Alliance ruled out any linkage, and in mid-January the Greeks began their pullout from Korcia. Left behind were members of the so-called "Sacred Legion," irregulars of all kinds including volunteers from Crete, but with Greek officers. Clashes with the Albanians, delays and excuses continued until the end of April when Athens announced that the withdrawal had been completed. But an underground force remained in the region. The Dutch gendarmerie, which was formed at this time, continued to insist that the Greeks had left troops behind.

Albania's new institutions were launched, but bumpily. The creation of a National Bank collided with the Entente's insistence that all the institutions "should be international in character and as such subject to the supervision of European governments." France specifically objected to the fact that the bank's two appointed vice presidents were respectively from Italy and Austria-Hungary. In other areas things went more smoothly. Twenty officers from the Netherlands plus an equal number of non-commissioned officers under the command of General De Weer arrived in Albania charged with organizing the national gendarmerie.

The Reign of the Prince of Wied

The search for a prince for Albania was launched immediately in accordance with the decision of the Ambassadors' Conference. It was a tried solution to an old problem. In the 19th century the Powers had more than once dipped into the rich reserve of Europe's small principalities to find rulers for new, breakaway states that had once been part of the crumbling Ottoman Empire. The best sources were the small German dynasties now subsumed into the larger German states, and surviving in all but name to provide eligible husbands on the royal marriage circuit.

Candidates had to be acceptable to all the Powers, obviously, and could not belong to a powerful reigning house, or one with a direct interest in the region. Past selections had always been Christians: Protestant or Catholic had without difficulty switched to the Orthodox faith of their new kingdoms or principalities. Albania presented a novel and different situation in that the population was predominantly Muslim.

The decision has a contemporary ring to it. Today's international organizations—the United Nations, NATO, the European Union, the Conference for Security and Cooperation in Europe (CSCE), the G8—have revived the practice of naming a high official who is an expression of their combined will. A "Special Representative of the Secretary General," or "senior administrator," or "personal representative" is appointed to a newly created state or an area in conflict such as—then as now—the Balkans to represent the authority of the international community in expectation of the time when the region under such control is capable of self-government.

In such cases an important part of the appointee's role is to assist in the development of democratic political institutions and an efficient administration, and strengthen internal security.

Following the London Conference the Powers were like matchmaking uncles looking for a suitable husband for a favorite niece. The selection involved intense, complex consultations. Close attention had to be paid to the delicate balance of interests between the Powers themselves. But as in many arranged marriages the "bride's" wishes were not consulted. The list of possible suitors was a long one. Already in March 1912, the Duke of Montpensier, Ferdinand of Bourbon-Orléans, had arrived in Valona on an English yacht and proclaimed himself a candidate for the Albanian title. He was well received by the Albanians, and when he set off to seek support in Rome, Paris, Vienna, and London he was accompanied by Isa Boletini, the Albanian partisan hero who had fought for the inclusion of Kosovo into Albania that same year, and would be killed in a firefight with Montenegrin forces in Podgorica in 1915. The time was not yet ripe for Montpensier, and later his cause was superseded by events.

Besides Montpensier, the initial list of "suitors" under consideration included the German Prince Mauritz von Schaumburg-Lippe, and Duke Karl von Urach; Prince Ghika of Romania (who later became a Roman Catholic bishop); Roland Bonaparte, descendant of Napoleon I; the Count of Turin, a member of the Italian royal House of Savoy; Arthur, Duke of Connaught, third son of Queen Victoria; Aladro Castriota, a descendant of Skanderbeg who lived in Italy. The Sublime Porte, in consideration of the fact that the majority of Albanians were Muslims, put forward three Muslim princes, Burham Eddin and Abdul Mejid belonging to the Ottoman dynasty, and Prince Ahmed Fuad, Pasha of Egypt, a descendent of Mohammed Ali, and therefore himself of Albanian origin.

Some encountered the objections of one or other of the Powers for different reasons and fell by the wayside, others expressed no interest in such a chancy undertaking. Ismail

Kemal and the members of the provisional government intimated to the Powers and to Constantinople that they preferred a European prince, so the choice narrowed down to a Western candidate to rule the new state.

With time running out the choice was left to Austria-Hungary and Italy who agreed on a German prince who was a Protestant, and thus unconnected with the religious disputes between Muslim and Orthodox Christian Albanians. This was Wilhelm of Wied,[5] and news of his appointment leaked out even before he had formally accepted the post. At the beginning of 1914 he let it be known that he had chosen Durrës as his capital.

Wilhelm of Wied was a captain on the German General Staff, a soldier with a strong sense of honor but no experience in either diplomacy or government, yet he was about to embark on an adventure full of uncertainty that would require exceptional talent and a generous dollop of luck. Prince Wilhelm's candidacy had the active backing of King Carol of Romania, at the insistence of his wife Queen Elizabeth, the prince's aunt. Elizabeth had a great affection for her nephew. A well-known writer under the pseudonym Carmen Sylva, she embarked on an image building campaign on his behalf turning out rhapsodic articles about his scholastic diligence, his physical prowess, his equestrian skill and his gifts as a military strategist. In one adoring piece she wrote that, "When they saw him in his white uniform of an officer in the Imperial Guard, with the silver eagle, the Romanians immediately dubbed him Lohengrin." As a student at Jena "he was always seen with a book with his fingers flipping the pages." She wrote that Wied "lifted up a fellow officer with one hand." The Princess of Wied also came in for her share of praise: She was artistic and musical having "inherited from her Romanian grandmother her southern character and her love for Latin countries."

In an article entitled "Wilhelm the Wise" published shortly after the prince accepted the throne, Carmen Sylva addresses Wied's new subjects, rejoicing that "the unfortunare Albanian people whom neither the Romans nor the Turks had succeeded in dominating have been given a protector who understands you and loves you, and who will protect your property and your lives."

The Italian press jumped on the bandwagon and lavished praise on "the ruler chosen by Europe" and reproduced with further embellishments profiles of the virtually unknown prince. Carmen Sylva's articles were prominently displayed in the Italian periodicals together with stories of an exemplary childhood and youth.

Kaiser Wilhelm II was less enthusiastic in his assessment of his cousin's abilities, and was reported at the time to have advised him not to accept the post. This was immediately denied, however. It was true that the Kaiser had pointed out the difficulties when the prince was first approached; but once

The Prince of Wied in military uniform.

Wied had accepted, the Kaiser had done nothing to reverse his decision. In his memoirs, written after the events in Albania and the First World War Wilhelm II expressed considerable doubt of Wilhelm of Wied's ability to govern, but it must be said that he was himself scarcely the best qualified to judge on that score.

Monsignor Fan Noli, the Orthodox cleric who was one of the leading figures in subsequent political developments, was to write with more sympathy and wisdom that the Prince of Wied "could only be criticized for not being capable of performing miracles."

In his own memoirs Wilhelm of Wied repeatedly complained that Italian, Russian and French intrigue and the plots of those whom they protected, plus "Greece's ability to

Queen Elisabeth of Romania with her niece, the Princess of Wied.

create mischief with impunity" and the "neutrality" of Britain and Germany, combined to undermine his mission and to seal the fate of his brief reign. He tried to explain Wilhelm II's coolness as the result of the emperor's dislike for Albania, and his Greek sympathies, influenced by his sister, the queen of Greece, and his brother-in-law King Constantine.

In a letter to the English historian Joseph Swire, the prince blamed the situation in Europe for the failure of his reign in Albania. When the Italo-Austrian cooperation failed and "the climate of preserving peace became one of preparing for war," the very foundation of his mission collapsed. "In normal circumstances," he added, "neither Essad nor the poor deluded rebels would have dared to oppose the European decision."

On February 6, the Prince of Wied was authorized by Italy and Austro-Hungary to notify Russian, French and British ambassadors in Berlin that he was ready to assume the Albanian throne, and on February 21 he received an Albanian delegation in Neuwied and accepted their offer to become their ruler.

Two months elapsed between the Powers' offer to Prince Wilhelm and his acceptance of the Albanian throne, and another two weeks after that before his departure for Durrës. But the unrest increased, foreshadowing the tensions to come. The prince would have preferred to postpone his arrival until his appointment had gained a greater degree of public acceptance, but Berchtold pressed him to depart at once for Albania, where, by the day, the situation was becoming more complex. Other European capitals shared this view. The Greeks, though, did not favor his swift assumption of power. They feared that it would be followed by a European military intervention in territories recently claimed from the Abanians.

In Valona and Elbasan the unrest continued intermittently. In the south, Greece ignored the International Commission's requests to withdraw, and the injunctions of the Powers and continued its occupation of Albanian areas. In Valona, the temporary seat of government, the intrigue among Albanian leaders was continuous, while Turkish agents fomented discontent among the Muslim population at the choice of a prince who was both a foreigner and a Christian.

There was a strong rivalry between Ismail Kemal, the head of the provisional government and Essad Pasha,[6] the president of the senate. In a commentary in *Illustrazione Italiana* headlined "Turbulent Eve of a New Reign" Gino Berti pulls no punches in his account of Essad's bloody past and current intrigues: "Astute, daring, hardly the very model of a loyal subject" he was leader of the "Muslim party" that had lost a round in the game against the Powers, but remained determined to win political power "if it was the will of Allah and Essad Pasha."

The conflict between the two figures erupted when an attempted pro-Turkish coup was defeated at the last minute, but not before the provisional government had been forced to declare a state of emergency. The failed coup by Bekit Aga was intended to overturn the decisions of the London conference and offer the crown to Izzet Pasha, a former Turkish minister of war of Albanian origin, even though he didn't speak the language. Izzet denied any implication in the coup, but the European press had little doubt, based on the evidence, that the Ottoman Empire was behind the coup, and eventually implicated both Essad and Ismail Kemal, both of whom also rejected any involvement. The plot started the earliest rumors that the Prince of Wied had renounced the Albanian throne, a speculation that was to recur intermittently until the end.

Bekir was immediately put on trial behind closed doors. The court was presided over by Gen. De Weer. The trial produced evidence of Turkish involvement, and seized documents cast considerable suspicion on Essad. Bekir was senenced to death, but the Control Commission decided to stay the execution and await the prince's arrival.

Albanians landing in the Italian port of Brindisi brought news of a country in deep ferment, and it was said that Prince Wilhelm "would find no subjects." The main objections were his Christian religion, and his decision to choose Durrës as the capital, which had "offended" other major cities. A report in *Il Giornale di Sicilia* of Jan 13-14 was headlined, "Albania in Flames? Grave News from Valona and Brindisi."

Meanwhile, Wied' s procrastination in leaving for Albania began to draw criticisim. Several times the papers reported his impending departure, but each time it was postponed. Articles in the press began to urge the prince to go to Durrës as quickly as possible, "so that the population will see the wishes of the (European) Powers respected." The *Giornale di Sicilia* had no illusion that the prince's life would be "unhappy and difficult," but the paper assured him that it would follow developments "with admiration, sympathy, and anxiety."

If the prince was having second thoughts about his acceptance to rule Albania, interviews with leading Albanians in the Viennese paper *Zeit* can have done little to dispel his hesitation. There were first of all complaints that in choosing a Christian prince the Powers had disregarded Albanian preferences. Others warned ominously that the public celebrations to welcome Prince Wilhelm would be "disturbed by rifle fire." They said fifty-thousand Albanians would be on hand "virtually all of them armed, and one never knows…" One official deplored the prince's delay in arriving in Albania, but noted that he had already sent ahead five hundred packing cases of personal items and household goods; he had also sent his doctor "to review medical conditions." Another noted that the prince "had let it be known that he would surround himself solely with Germans and English people, and would distance from his court members of the old Albanian aristocracy."

By now the situation of the provisional government had become untenable, and on February 15 Ismail Kemal asked the Control Commission to take over. The Powers agreed, and thanked the old patriot very warmly. The latter left for Europe having first sent a message to San Giuliano and Berchtold imploring them "to help these courageous and unhappy people to defend their rights too little respected by their enemies."

With the departure of Ismail Kemal and Essad, who had promised to resign along with Kemal, a period of relative calm could have followed. But it turned out that Essad did not resign claiming as his justification for staying on that Ismail had in effect been removed from office, and moreover that the Bekir plot had not been totally suppressed and still constituted a danger to the country. Essad let it be known that he planned to go to the Prince of Wied and personally offer him the Albanian throne. The Control Commission gave in, appointing him head of the delegation that was to invite Wied to become ruler of Albania, but insisted that Essad submit his resignation prior to his departure. Chalk one up for the Pasha!

On the ground, the Dutch officers had made steps in organizing the gendarmerie. Major Thomson[7] was responsible for forming the units stationed in the south. He told them he

Rome: The Prince of Wied meeting with the Marquis of San Giuliano.

"entrusted the independence of the nation to their patriotism." There were still financial problems because the promised 75 million franc loan from the Powers had still not arrived, and Austria-Hungary and Italy had stepped in with a temporary advance, but it was only five million francs each.

The prince had begun to create his court and was planning official visits to the Powers that had nominated him. First stop on his itinerary was Rome then Vienna, followed by London and Paris. He was trying to maintain an equilibrium in his relations with Austria-Hungary and Italy while at the same time not neglecting the members of the Entente. In Durrës, work had begun on the restoration of a modest sized, somewhat rundown palace that was to be the seat of the Prince of Albania. Restorers arrived from Berlin. From Vienna came furniture and fittings sent by the prince. Photographs show an old Turkish Konak[8] being converted into a modest residence, but it was a start.

Also due to arrive in the new Albanian capital were the prince's "seventeen horses and his three red hunting outfits," reported the magazine *Illustrazione Italiana* not without irony. But the same publication had hailed the prince on setting foot in Rome on February 11 as "a distinguished personality of refined taste and a magnificent gentleman," and had published his portrait with San Giuliano on its cover. The Italian press generally welcomed the prince with sympathy and a certain smug satisfaction that, "Italian policy had prevailed in the formation of the new state."

The prince had an audience with King Vittorio Emanuele III who invested him with the order of Saints Maurizio and Lazzaro, but one publication commented that Wied's trip to Rome was also "a kind of moral investiture." Wied also met Prime Minister Giolitti and had a long discussion with San Giuliano. *Il Giornale d'Italia* saw the prince's stay in Rome as more than a courtesy visit. Wied, the paper said, had had "substantive meetings which would serve as guidelines in his difficult task of government, in which he faced a thousand difficulties not only due to conditions in Albania, but also to the diplomatic situation which requires a fine sense of balance."

The paper hoped that Wied's talks in Rome had shown the prince that "the road to Durrës passed through Rome and through Vienna." *La Tribuna* was more optimistic. "After the convulsions in Valona and Durrës there is a new calm in Albania as the country waits full of hope for the sovereign chosen by the Powers. The Prince of Wied is surrounded by the best elements of the new state. The harmony that prevails would almost seem incredible."

Everything was ready for the great adventure.

The devil, however, is in the detail–and quickly showed himself. In the wake of such optimism, the prince completed his goodwill tour, returning to Neuwied and then sailing to Durrës in the Austrian Imperial navy's yacht Taurus, specially fitted out for the journey and escorted by an international naval squadron. It was arranged that the prince would board the Taurus in Trieste–and there was the rub. By tradition no unit of the Italian navy could visit Trieste, and none had done so since 1866, the year of the sea battle between the Italian and Austrian fleets off the island of Lissa in the Adriatic.

Anticipating a major row, Captain Castoldi—the Italian officer "attached to the Ministry of Foreign Affairs for diplomatic missions," who jointly with the Austrian diplomat Buchberger formed the prince's political staff[9] —tried to minimize the issue, stressing the importance of Italo-Austrian cooperation and the cordial relationship between the respective capitals. But the political fallout both in Trieste and Rome was such that the Italian Ministry of Marine announced that the navy battleship Quarto, assigned to escort the prince, would join the Taurus at sea instead of joining the squadron in Trieste.

On February 12, Essad left Albania on his solemn mission after making a speech praising the prince. The following day – three days after the prince's own visit to Rome – Essad declared to journalists without batting an eyelid that "only a few mischief makers could have tried to make Europe believe for one moment that there was dissent in Albania." He expressed pride for and gratitude in the mission he had undertaken. "The delegation I head reflects the first expression of

Albanian collective conscience since Skanderbeg." The deputation stopped in Cologne to formulate the protocol for offering the prince the crown. One problem to be resolved was the question of title in translation. Essad was to address the prince as Mbret, an all-embracing term in Albanian meaning sire, prince, king, or sovereign. But how would the term be translated in French – prince, or king of Albania? The crown specially made for him by a leading European jeweler didn't provide much guidance. It consisted of two gold circles studded with turquoise surmounted, not by a cross or crescent, but by a more neutral star.

On February 22, the Rhineland Prussian town of Neuwied, flag-decked and festive, with a triumphal arch set up facing Wied castle, received the top-hatted Albanian delegates. The prince greeted Essad Pasha who in turn formally offered him the crown of a "free and independent Albania." Essad went on to assure the prince that "Albanians without exception

The cover of *La Tribuna Illustrata* showing the Prince of Wied being offered the crown of Albania.

would be loyal subjects of Your Highness and always ready to support your efforts to lead Albania to a prosperous and glorious future," and ended with the shout of "Long live the Mbret of Albania."

The prince, replying in German, accepted the crown of a country which, "after numerous struggles and difficulties has reconquered its freedom," and expressed his commitment to the well being of the Albanian people. The prince did not hide his initial hesitation to accept so great a responsibility, but said he welcomed the assurances of loyalty and support of the Albanian people.

On the homeward journey to Albania Essad Pasha stopped in Vienna where on March 1 he was received by the old emperor and by Berchtold with the same level of formality that he had been in Rome, Berchtold conferring on him the Cross of the Order of Francis Joseph. Not to be outdone, the Italian ambassador, Avarna, invited Essad to the Italian Embassy and designated him a knight of the Crown of Italy.

En route to Durrës, Prince William stopped over in Trieste where he was warmly received on March 5, by the Austrian authorities and the Albanian Catholic dignitaries with ties to

Durrës: Bishop Caciorri shown with a military chaplain (detail).

Austria, Archbishop Bianchi and the influential Bishop Caciorri (Kacori). Following a visit to the Miramar castle, the prince boarded the Taurus accompanied by his wife and staff and set sail with an international naval escort.

The prince landed at Durrës on March 7, 1914 to a festive welcome of flags and a 21-gun royal salute from naval ships in harbor and a shore battery in the capital. A raft of dignitaries greeted the royal couple, including the prefect of Durrës, General De Weer, commander of the gendarmerie, and other Albanian officials; Italian and Austrian troops furnished a guard of honor, and the band played the new national anthem of Albania composed by the Italian musician Evemero Nardella. Throughout the city there were enthusiastic demonstrations, but not—noted Chekrezi—in support of the Mbret but rather in celebration of Albania's freedom from foreign domination. Groups had come from every part of the country, and from Albanian enclaves abroad including the *arbereshe*, the ethnic Albanian minority in southern Italy.

The prince marked the occasion by releasing a surprising statement. "My reign will be neither absolute nor constitutional," he declared. "I will exercise my will in the organization of the state, but the country will play its part through the actions of a Senate half of which will be elected by myself and half by the people."

The festivities for the sovereign's arrival lasted one week, culminating on the 16th with a solemn Te Deum in the Orthodox cathedral, but with the participation of the Catholic archbishop of Scutari, Monsignor Sereggi (Serreqi). The prince wore for the first time the blue uniform of a general of the Albanian army; the princess wore a violet dress.

Emperor Wilhelm II issued a proclamation addressed to the Albanians, saying he expected "that all would rally round your king and work with us for the fulfillment of (Albanian) national aspirations." The prince immediately formed his government: Turkhan Pasha Permeti, a former ambassador of the Ottoman Empire, was appointed prime minister (president of the Council) and foreign minister of independent Albania, Essad Pasha Toptani, who was commissioned as

The Reign of the Prince of Wied

Durrës: Baron Buchberger and Captain Castoldi, advisers to the Prince of Wied.

Essad Pasha Toptani, minister of war and interior minister at the start of the prince's reign.

general, got the war and interior portfolios and was responsible for national security, Mufid bey Libohova was made minister of justice and religious affairs. The royal household also took form with Trotha, Castoldi, and Buchberger as the prince's counselors, and the Englishman D.Eaton Armstrong as private secretary. Three Albanians completed the small team: Sami bey Vrioni, chamberlain, and aides-de-camp, Ekrem bey Libohova and Selim bey Vassa.

Yet Wied began his reign with a decision of questionable wisdom: having formed his government he sent the International Control Commission, designated by the London Conference to assist him and oversee the civil administration and its finances, to Valona thus removing a potentially useful intermediary with the chancelleries of the European Powers.

To judge from the photographs and press reports, the European expatriate colony enjoyed an active social life. Elegant officers and their ladies were shown at receptions, tennis parties, and open-air cafes. For Princess Sophia there were evenings of water music performed by musicians on the royal yacht.

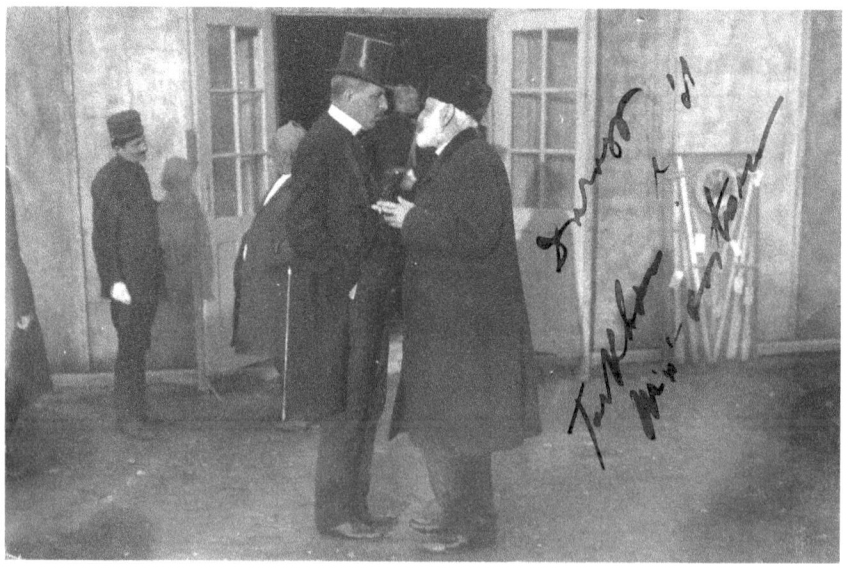

The Austro-Hungarian minister in Albania, Löwenthal, listens to Albanian Prime Minister Turkhan Pasha (detail).

Mirditi leader Preng Bib Doda.

The Italian naval squadron commanded by the Duke of Abruzzi paid an official visit to Durrës and Valona, hosting the prince for breakfast in the flagship Regina Elena. Then came a royal dinner attended by all the members of the government at which the Prince of Wied conferred on the duke the first decoration of his reign, the Albanian Eagle.

But the underlying unrest quickly came to the surface with an incursion in the south by Greek "Epiroti Volunteers" who attacked the gendarmerie. The latter, however, held their own supported by forces sent from the north by Bib Doda, "prince" of the Mirditi. Refugees began to flow in from Tepelene and Argirocastro. In Argirocastro, the gendarmes had surrounded the town's Epiroti quarter and found themselves facing regular Greek troops commanded by General Papoulias. The prince lodged a protest against the Greek violence with the Powers. Essad apparently even proposed leading an expedition of 25,000 men into the Epirus region.

The Powers charged the International Commission with negotiating a cessation of hostilities with the Greek authorities and with the Epiroti of Zographos; and on May 17 the Commission's Corfu "dispositions" were delivered to the European capitals as guarantors of any agreement. These "dispositions" were approved on July 12. They called for the withdrawal of Greek forces, but the Epiroti gained a measure of autonomy in that they were allowed to form their own local gendarmerie (with Dutch officers) for exclusive use in Korcia and Argirocastro, and composed of volunteers already under arms.

Moreover, the Albanian government was charged with appointing Christian governors for the area under agreement, and with holding elections for local councils. Freedom of worship was assured, and the Greek language was to be taught in the schools and admitted for use in the courts and the administration.

Because the Epirus crisis had major international implications, it overshadowed two other serious contemporary situations, Serbian annexation of Kosovo and regions of the north annexed by Montenegrins. When, in mid-April, Serbia and Montenegro began to annex territory assigned to them they ran into strong resistance. The Albanians demanded schooling in their own language: the government in Belgrade refused, imposing Serbian as the sole language in the schools. The Serbians suppressed the resulting unrest by destroying more than a thousand homes and killing several hundred women and children. The Montenegrins moved into their newly acquired territory with such force that many Albanians fled as homes were burned. The English Colonel Phillips, commander of the International Force in Skhoder dispatched 600 international troops led by a German major to maintain order.

"The Events at Durazzo"

By May 19 the Prince's government was facing its first serious crisis. It started as a minor peasant unrest, but within a few hours mixed signals and residual suspicions had transformed it into a full scale turf battle between the international gendarmerie and the Albanian government. By the time the dust had settled Essad Pasha had been arrested, accused of treason, and exiled.

It had started on May 17 in Shijak, a village between Tirana and Durrës. A group of armed Albanians clashed with a gendarmerie detachment. The Albanians were apparently demanding exemption from compulsory conscription (and possibly the removal of Essad). They seemed bent on going to Durrës to make their case.

Essad Pasha ordered Major Johan Sluys to deploy two machine-guns on the road to defend the capital. But Sluys refused, saying that he only obeyed orders from the Prince himself, or from his own Dutch superiors. It was an affront that the minister of war–recently promoted to general by the Prince himself–and an influential tribal chief and pasha of the Ottoman Empire could not possibly tolerate, and Essad took his protest to the Prince, demanding the major's immediate dismissal.

Wilhelm of Wied was not inclined to lose a loyal officer and refused to fire the Dutch major. Instead, acting also on the advice of the Italian minister Aliotti, he ordered Sluys on indefinite leave to be followed by a transfer to Shkoder. Essad promptly resigned from the government.

The Prince refused to accept Essad's resignation, but even so the hapless minister suffered a remarkable reversal of fortune. Major Sluys turned out to be a formidable enemy. His retaliation was to convince the Prince that Essad was actually a traitor, and the Prince ordered his arrest. The minister increased the size of his bodyguard and prepared for a confrontation. Amid growing tension, Prince Wilhelm requested protection. Italian and Austrian marines were landed from the combined fleet to defend the royal palace and the various legations. On May 19, Sluys, who had been ordered to carry out the arrest, surrounded Essad's house. After a brief fire fight, in which the gendarmerie even brought up and opened fire with a field piece, the pasha gave himself up. His papers were seized (the press spoke of "packets of letters"), and Essad himself was detained on the Austro-Hungarian warship Szigervar.

Once accomplished, the arrest created a political dilemma. A public trial could ignite strong public reaction. On the other hand, for the Prince to let the matter drop would surely be interpreted as a sign of weakness.

Again on the advice of Aliotti and the Romanian envoy Burghele, dean of the diplomatic corps, the Prince decided on a compromise. There would be no trial, but Essad would be sent into exile. Essad was escorted onto an Italian passenger ship, publicly protesting his innocence, and sailed for Italy on May 21. Before departing he signed a commitment on his honor never to return and not to involve himself in "any internal or external agitation."

In Rome, San Giuliano told Parliament in effect that he had no information concerning the incident, causing such resentment that for a while the press carried strong hints of the impending resignation of the minister of foreign affairs. The Albanian prime minister, who was on a fund-raising tour of key European capitals, professed ignorance of whatever it was, Essad may or may not have been plotting.

What lay behind Essad's ouster–an Italian conspiracy, or on the contrary a subtle maneuver by Vienna to remove a key political figure because of his close ties with Italy? An official

Durrës.

inquiry that was supposed to shed light on "the events of May 19" never took place because, as San Giuliano argued in a note sent to Italian embassies, any investigation of the matter would have undermined the Prince's prestige. The minister further asserted his belief in Berchtold's good faith, "even if it is believed that an inquiry would produce proof that would render Austrian influence [in this matter] virtually undeniable."

But in Durrës problems between Italy and Austria had become acute. Close to despair, San Giuliano turned for help to Berlin.

Would the Germans lean on Vienna "to give its legation clear and precise instructions" on Italian-Austrian relations?

Vienna's response was to shift the blame onto the Prince, or at any rate onto his court. "Recent developments in Durrës were the work of the prince's court and the Dutch officers. Austria-Hungary had no part in them, neither directly or indirectly." The foreign minister "had always held the view that it was best to "manage" Essad Pasha rather than to confront him, and this had always been [the foreign minister's] approach." Furthermore, it was pointed out to Ambassador Avarna that, "it has to be acknowledged that the anti-Italian movement in Scutari, in Durrës, and in Valona, was the result of a campaign favoring Essad in our press; and also the result of Aliotti's recent actions."

In Rome and Vienna the dramatic incident provided ammunition for a lengthy exchange of broadsides between Italian and Austrian commentators and editorial writers, each side viewing it as the other country's mischief. In Vienna, Essad was seen as little more than an agent for the Italians, the Serbs, the Turks, and possibly the Greeks as well. In Rome, the pasha was the victim of an Albanian nationalist plot organized by Austria, "to destroy our position in Durrës," as more than one editorial expressed it.

Colorful accounts of the siege and Essad's arrest filled the newspapers: the number of artillery rounds fired; Essad's surrender; his wife imploring the gendarmerie to have pity on her husband; Essad handing over his pistol but asking to be allowed to keep his sword; his repeated statements of loyalty to Prince Wilhelm. But the real Essad was an ambivalent character, an unscrupulous, ambitious schemer. Following the Prince's departure a few months later he would be back, and would seize control of Durrës and the central region. (In 1920, he would be assassinated in Paris.)

Essad's removal did not restore peace in Albania. In Durrës, the ferment and the general uncertainty did not abate; and Italian and Austrian sailors continued to guard the Prince's palace. Worse still, on May 20 a major uprising had begun in central Albania where Turkish agents had been active among the Muslim population. It was led by the mufti of Tirana, and spearheaded by Islamist fundamentalists from Bosnia who had sought refuge in Albania under the Porte during the Austrian occupation of Bosnia-Herzegovina. There were some who felt that the timing was not coincidental, and saw Essad's hand in it.

In fact, it did not take long for the insurgents in Tirana

to join forces with the protesting peasants in Shijak, a few kilometers away. The insurrection threatened Durrës and the Prince's combined armed forces—the international contingents, the Albanian regulars, and the volunteers—were mobilized to defend the city.

A detachment of the gendarmerie led by a Dutch major and supported by Isa Boletini and his Kosovar fighters occupied the commanding heights of Rashbull overlooking Durrës. Captain Jan Saar, another Dutch officer, was dispatched to Tirana with fifty gendarmes, and two hundred Malissori and Mirditi, all Catholics, the latter headed by Simon Doda. Prince Sturdza, an attaché from the Romanian Legation, with a company of artillery, completed the meager column.

The defense plan turned into a fiasco due to a breakdown in communication between the Dutch. When Saar's force arrived in Shijak, the Malissori refused to fight. Saar sought further orders by telegraph from Gen. De Weer whose reply was to proceed as planned, without the recalcitrant Catholic tribesmen. Leaving Shijak on the Tirana road Saar found himself facing a strong force of Bosnian Islamists. He gave the order to open fire, but the Bosnians outnumbered his gendarmes and quickly surrounded them. Saar fought on until half his men were lost and the ammunition ran out, and then surrendered and was taken prisoner.

Saar's defeat and surrender were a humiliation for the government. Far worse, the Shijak debacle triggered a full scale tribal uprising, and the earlier scattered incidents were transformed into full scale insurgency. As a gesture of respect to the newly arrived Prince the Albanian tribes, following a long tradition, had declared a truce of honor in the complex pattern of blood feuds and vendettas that conditioned relationships among a large part of the population. But Captain Saar had broken that truce by ordering his troops to open fire on the Bosnian Islamists: the foreign, Christian Prince had proved unworthy of the tribute that had been paid him. In an instant all of central Albania was up in arms. The Ottoman flag was raised in Tirana and Kavaja; loyalists were imprisoned.

The insurgents, now greatly increased, occupied the heights above Durrës and on May 23 began their advance on the capital itself. By the afternoon the fate of the city seemed sealed. "A night of anguish and terror in the Albanian capital" read the banner headline in the *Giornale di Sicilia*. Bands of rebels with no cohesive leadership had approached to within a few kilometers of the city limits. European residents took refuge in their respective embassies hoping to be evacuated by friendly ships.

The main defense of the city consisted of 150 men under the command of Major Lucas Roelfsema (who was taken in the battle) and of Baron Gumpelberg, "a German adventurer." The international naval squadron had orders not to intervene unless Prince Wilhelm himself needed to be rescued.

Aliotti's account to Rome of the dramatic sequence of events of May 24 was published the following day in the Italian press. The Italian minister described how, as the rebels advanced, the Prince's personal bodyguard of Catholic Malissori led by two priests had fled. The Prince had sent a leading Albanian figure, the aged Mehmet Pasha Draga, to parley with the rebels, but the latter failed to make any headway with the rebels. The panic in the capital was indescribable. Aliotti said he made two proposals to the Prince. 1) Remove the Malissori "whose continued presence was seen as a provocation by the Muslim insurgents;" and 2) "send the Princess and their two young children to safety and then withdraw the [Italian and Austrian] sailors to prevent serious incidents." But the Princess refused to be parted from her husband, so the decision was taken that the Prince himself should, as a temporary measure, also embark on the Misurata.[10]

After some hesitation, Löwenthal, the Austrian minister in Durrës, also backed the proposal and the Albanian royal couple left the palace and boarded the Italian ship. They were accompanied by Admiral Trifari, commanding the Italian squadron, and the diplomatic representatives of Italy, Austria, and Romania, and the Albanian Minister of Justice. The Malissori bodyguard refused to quit the shore until the Prince was safely on board. Then launches transferred them

Scutari: Italo Sulliotti, correspondent of *La Trubuna Illustrata* with Italian officers and another journalist.

to the Szigervar, the same Austro-Hungarian warship that had briefly been Essad's floating prison. They boarded—as one inspired reporter put it—"slowly and in silence, the sun flashing on their gold braided uniforms, on their silver-handled pistols, and on the steel barrels of their rifles, but on their faces the sorrow of defeat."

The Prince's stay on the Misurata lasted only a few hours, but it cost him dear in terms of the blow to his prestige, in Albania, throughout Europe, and even in Austria. The press accused him of running scared, but that was unfair: he was a soldier and a man of honor.

The magazine *L'Illustrazione Italiana* dismissed the crisis as "operatic." Italo Sulliotti, the correspondent of *La Tribuna Illustrata*, later wrote scathingly of the embarkation in a book on Wied's short-lived reign. The Princess, "haughty, her lips pursed in anger," came on board with a retinue of ladies-in-waiting and chambermaids. "One of the maids lovingly carried a small dog in her arms." Observing the scene, Sulliotti relates, a naval officer murmured, "It's the flight to Varennes."

With the Albanian royals safely out of harm's way a fresh parley with the insurgents was organized. Col. Muricchio and five members of the Control Commission made their way to Shijak under a flag of truce—and the flag of Italy. They visited the wounded members of the gendarmerie, who were then released, and then listened to the grievances of the rebels. According to press accounts, the main complaints were that the government "had done nothing for Albania;" and Prince Wilhelm had broken the truce by sending troops to Shijak and opening fire on the insurgents. If they could not have a government "from Europe," they said, they might just as well return to Turkish rule. Later, rebel representatives met with the envoys of Italy and Romania, together with some members of the Control Commission and Baron Berger from the Austro-Hungarian legation, (Löwenthal, the Austrian minister, had apparently remained on the Szigervar and was sharply rebuked by the Hungarian press for doing so).

As the ever informative Aliotti reported to Rome, the in-

The yacht Misurata in Durrës Harbor.

surrection had been spontaneous, and was motivated by religious concerns. The rebel representatives undertook not to enter the capital– but only if a delegation was received by the Prince. And they threatened to shoot their prisoners unless the Prince agreed to their demand by the following morning. As a pre-condition they also demanded a commitment that the government would never fire on them again - which was tantamount to demanding its surrender.

What is most interesting is the way these developments are transformed in the hands of an eminent historian like Swire into an Italian plot, as was the earlier Essad conspiracy. For example, in recounting Aliotti's audience with the Prince on the tumultuous afternoon of May 23, and the minister's advice that the royal family should take refuge on the Misurata to avoid a massacre, Swire suggests that Aliotti deliberately exaggerated the danger in the full knowledge that for Wied to leave would undermine his political and personal prestige. Swire also says that Aliotti left Captain Castoldi behind at the palace with instructions to examine the Prince's personal papers.

In Swire's version of events, Prince Wilhelm escorted his family on board the Misurata intending to return at once to the palace. But the ship had immediately raised anchor and sailed for the roads to take station on the rest of the squadron, leaving the prince (Swire wrote) "a virtual prisoner in the hands of the Italians."

By his own account Aliotti sent Admiral Trifari to brief the Prince on board the Misurata, and to advise him to return to the palace. In the evening the Prince and Princess disembarked, leaving their children and most of their household on board, and Italian sailors once more took up protective positions around the palace. The squadron remained on full alert as the situation seemed to be worsening.

In Shkoder, a group of Catholics staged a demonstration in support of Prince Wilhelm of Wied. From all accounts the demonstrators were pro-Austrian and the action had apparently been inspired by the Austrian consul. "The Christians have no support whatsoever," the Italian consul, Galli,

Admiral Trifari with Captain Castoldi and Baron Aliotti (detail).

reported to Rome dismissively. He cautioned his Austrian colleague that Christian activism in the crisis did little more than increase the level of Muslim discontent. In their search for a cause the Muslims had now added Essad's expulsion to their list of complaints, even though he had been a member of the government and as such shared in the responsibility for the perceived injustices that had triggered the disturbances in the first place. But Essad's arrest and subsequent exile were now seen as an insult against a fellow Muslim. From Kosovo and Djakova thousands now set out for Tirana to reinforce the insurgents. But in Alessio, groups of Catholic Mirditi and Malissori tribesmen also assembled, and their mood was equally combative.

Members of the Control Commission traveled around the country to talk to the insurgents. On May 28 the Austrian commissioner was in Shijak. This time the demands mainly reflected conventional local concerns—improved infrastructure, more schools, a gendarmerie; but they included a return to Albanian autonomy under Turkish suzerainty. The commissioners ruled out a return to Ottoman rule. Albania was now "under Europe's protection," he said. To show their

Durrës: The heliograph on the roof of the Austrian Legation (detail).

good faith, the insurgents released their prisoners, and actually handed back the artillery pieces captured in the fighting with the gendarmerie five days earlier. Such was the disarray in the international force that no transport was available to move the guns, which remained in Shijak. The rebels reclaimed them and later used them against Durrës. But the willingness to negotiate was not universal. In Kavaja, the rebels refused to have anything to do with representatives of the Prince's government.

At this point the Italian legation's relations with the Prince were seriously undermined by Austrian press reports that the Italians were, in effect, spying for the insurgents. In May the Austrian press had begun to hint at cloak-and-dagger activities by two Italian officers, Col. Muricchio and Captain Moltedo who were said to be passing on intelligence to the insurgents. The Viennese paper *Fremdenblatt* noted that the two officers had made "continuous trips in the area outside Tirana," and had furthermore refused to allow the Dutch gendarmerie to inspect the contents of some of the bags they had with them. The paper referred to a house occupied by an

Italian from which "Morse code signals" had been made with a flashlight or semaphore lamp, and were answered from the rebel lines.

Curiously, *Fremdenblatt* had anticipated a sequence of real events that further fueled the Prince's suspicions of Italian intentions. On June 5, the gendarmerie reported that there had indeed been an exchange of signals between a certain house and the Rashbull heights, which were held by the rebels. On Thomson's[11] orders, the gendarmerie occupied the house and arrested Muricchio, Moltedo, and a Professor Chinigò, seizing many documents. Chinigò was an expert on Albanian culture recently arrived in Durrës from Shkoder and working for the Italian government in the area of propaganda.

Aliotti immediately went into action, demanding the release of the two officers and the professor, together with an apology from the now Colonel Thomson. The Dutchman refused and instead produced witnesses and compromising documents found in the possession of the trio in detention.

The situation was explosive and needed to be defused quickly. Italy launched a vigorous political offensive on several fronts, and the worst was avoided. On June 7, the Albanian prime minister visited Aliotti to express his regrets, deplore the incident, and assure the envoy that the Albanian government had no intention of taking any action with regard to the accusations against Muricchio and Chinigò. The government subsequently withdrew the accusations in writing and offered reparations. Later still, Aliotti saw the Prince and–as he reported to Rome–the government "acknowledged that the Dutch (gendarmerie) colonel had behaved incorrectly, and promised full satisfaction." This came in the form of another letter from Prime Minister Turkhan Pasha to Aliotti stating that "there was nothing compromising in the papers that had been sequestered."

To San Giuliano, Aliotti flatly denied that "any Italian in Durrës" had spied for the insurgents. He believed the incident was the result of rumors spread by "nationalists and Austrian agents." He named "the notorious Biegeleben and one of the principal organizers of the Muricchio incident," a reference to the nephew of a senior official in the Ministry of Foreign Affairs in Vienna who had turned up in Albania as a volunteer and had been appointed chief of police in Durrës by the Prince. It was Biegeleben who had set up a system of signal lights on a house and Muricchio had been mistakenly identified with the arrangement.

To Aliotti's intense satisfaction, the German minister told him some days later that, "after carefully reviewing all the facts of the situation he had come to the conclusion that the Italian action had been loyal, logical and best suited to the serious situation in Albania." The minister had also indicated that Biegeleben's mysterious activities, as well as his background had worried the Germans.

It is possible that Colonel Thomson had been the victim of deliberate disinformation. He was involved in a similar incident (with the same result) when he arrested the mayor of Durrës, an individual of Montenegrin origin named Djurasković, apparently for making public statements against the government and particularly for declaring that the Prince's fate was sealed. But Djurasković was released following the intervention of the Russians.

Tired of the machinations swirling around him, Prince Wilhelm fired both his political counselors, Castoldi and Buchberger. Thomson and Aliotti pointedly ignored each other. The Italian threatened to request the Dutchman's recall, but the Albanians secured an extension of his stay until July 3 because an immediate change would endanger the security of the city. The decision was to prove fatal for the colonel. He was among the first casualties of the events at Durrës. In the absence of any progress on the political front the situation continued to deteriorate. In the atmosphere of growing discontent the rebel force in Shijak continued to grow. As its ranks swelled so did its boldness, and by the beginning of June the insurgents were calling outright for the Prince's abdication and his replacement with a Muslim head of state. If the European powers insisted on a Christian prince for Albania it could no longer be the Prince of Wied who had "fired on his people."

On June 4 the government declared a state of siege in Durrës, but it was not until dawn of June 15 that the insurgents attacked, forcing their way across the Legune bridge, and at the same time attacking from the hills. The Prince rode to the barracks of the Malissori and then inspected the group of houses where the defenders of the city had established their last line of defense. The garrison had been reinforced by foreign volunteers, including several German and Austrian reserve officers. It was these volunteers who manned the artillery and threw back the insurgent attack. The Shijak attackers were, of course, using the guns captured from Captain Saar at Shijak.

The Prince was among the defenders who received him warmly. Among the earliest casualties was Colonel Thomson[12] who died at an advance post as he encouraged the Albanian troops. With the news of his death the situation seemed to worsen, but Major Roelfsma assumed command and ordered the artillery into action, including a forward battery commanded by Prince Wilhelm himself.

Groups of the Prince's supporters went through the streets pressing able bodied men into service. The Italian sailors extended their defensive line from the palace to the Italian legation, where the Princess had sought shelter with her family. Simon Doda's Mirditi and the Kosovars led by Isa Boletini, taking advantage of the disarray among the insurgents, charged the trenches they had only recently abandoned, and recaptured them.

Meanwhile, another thousand (perhaps fifteen hundred) Mirditi sent by Bib Doda arrived in an Austrian ship led by their Catholic soldier-clerics, the bishops of Alessio and Zadrime, the notorious Bishop Caciorri,[13] a prelate who had come to Albania with Prince Wilhelm. Without the providential arrival of these reinforcements "the city would surely have been taken," reported the correspondent of the *Corriere della Sera*. On June 16 the rebels pulled back all along the line, but the attack was resumed the following day. The front page headline of *Il Giornale di Sicilia* read "A new dawn of bloodshed at the gates of Durazzo."

In a desperate effort to break the siege and push the insurgents towards Tirana, the government planned a surprise dawn attack against their positions on the Rashbull heights. On June 18 close to five thousand troops advanced on the enemy–six hours behind schedule because of disagreements between the Albanian commanders and their Dutch counterparts. The government troops were certainly not a force to be reckoned with, and the attack was doomed from the start. The tribal fighters were brave but undisciplined, and failed to coordinate their tactics with that of the regular troops. At first the latter moved forward without encountering any resistance, but then came under heavy fire from hidden rebel positions. Led by their priests, Mirditi tribesmen advanced towards Shijak with the Malissori deployed on their right flank. Here, too, there was little initial resistance, but then the enemy opened up a withering fire from the lateral hilltops and panic set in. As the tribesmen withdrew towards Durrës in confusion the insurgents counter attacked, and regained all their lost ground overlooking the city.

Aliotti to Rome on June 18: "The defeat of the government forces sent against the rebels was complete. The government has had an irreparable loss of prestige. There is no longer any hope of breaking through the enemy encircling the city. The Prince no longer makes decisions and his authority appears to be totally compromised."

Years later, the Prince of Wied would tell Swire that the insurgents' attack on the city had come "as a complete surprise to all–except the Italians who had been so sure of [the rebels'] success that the news of the fall of Durrës was published in the Italian press!" The Prince's allegations were unjustified, even though some episodes, notably Essad's arrest and the Muricchio/Chinigò incident have never been fully clarified. In truth, the Italian press never anticipated the fall of Durrës, even though reports from correspondents did tend to treat the impending collapse of the city's defenses as a foregone conclusion. On June 16, the *Corriere della Sera* informed its readers that "in a few hours Durrës will end its brave resistance," and on the same say the *Giornale d'Italia,* under the headline "Imminent Fall" quoted what the paper described as "an alarming telegram sent from Durrës" in which the paper's correspondent wrote, "Perhaps when this telegram is published the city will be in the hands of the insurgents." Their attack, he said, "is uninterrupted and violent."

But the rebels failed to press their advantage and on June 19 the Prince's capital was calm, and still in government hands. On the previous day, while the battle raged, Colonel Thomson

King Zog.

had been buried with full military honors. The burial rite was performed by the chaplain of the British warship Defence, which was part of the international maritime squadron along with units of the Italian and Austro-Hungarian fleets, a floating symbol of European support for Prince Wilhelm and his government. The Prince and Princess, the members of the Control Commission, members of the diplomatic corps, and the Italian and Austro-Hungarian admirals all attended the funeral of the fallen soldier.

Past differences were set aside and the Italian press reported that when Thomson was laid to rest "in the land for which he had died all present honored a man who had perhaps made more than one mistake, but had died doing his duty."

On June 20 the insurgents asked for a short cease-fire of two or three days to hold top level consultations. Despite objections from the Dutch officers, the government agreed to suspend operations until noon on June 24.

Despite the failure of the government's counterattack the Prince and his advisers still felt that the best strategy was the all-out suppression of the rebellion, arguing that the majority of the population had remained passive and had not joined the rebels. The next plan was a pincer attack with Bib Doda advancing from Alessio with five thousand men, a thousand-strong force massing between Berat, Elbasan and Valona, and Ahmed Zogu, the future King Zog, leading two thousand troops from Mat. Preparations for the surprise offensive took two weeks, during which time news of the government's intentions leaked out in the press. No wonder then that the insurgents were waiting. The Elbasan column of gendarmes was repulsed and forced to retreat, leaving two of its Dutch officers in rebel hands. The troops from Valona were also thrown back, and the Berat force drew back to Korcia. Bib Doda, who had managed to muster two thousand fighters instead of the expected five thousand, plus the Romanian diplomat Prince Sturdza commanding his artillery, parlayed with the insurgents instead of fighting them. His force dispersed and made its way back north. Sturdza was recalled to

Bucharest, and Romania rejected an appeal to send troops to Albania fearing objections from Serbia (but allowed volunteers). Zogu occupied Kruja, but did not engage the insurgents.

The insurrection was now in control of central and southern Albania. Prince Wilhelm on June 25 left Durrës on an Italian warship to visit Valona, which he found thronged with refugees from all over the country. On June 28, following another short cease fire, Colonel Phillips arrived from Shkoder at the head of the international force of British, French, and German troops, to reorganize the gendarmerie. Phillips also reopened what had been failed peace talks with five rebel leaders, including a Greek Orthodox cleric and a member of the Young Turks movement. The rebels were ready to negotiate most of the issues, but were immovable on one point: The Prince of Wied must leave Albania. The rebels agreed not to attack Durrës, but declared themselves determined not to lay down their arms until they had achieved their aims.

By the end of June it was clear that only Shkoder and Valona, in addition to the capital were under government control. Even so, Valona came under siege on June 29. Throughout Europe the press was filled with expressions of grave concern; and the Prince, now no longer a romantic figure, was everywhere blamed for the failure of the Powers' grand plan.

In Vienna the published view was that Wied would be forced to quit the Albanian throne because "the insurgents were masters of the situation and his position was now untenable." The paper *Die Zeit* stated bluntly that, "It would be best if Wilhelm, who had shown no talent, neither political or military, disappeared from the scene to avoid further bloodshed." In London the Prince's position was also seen as desperate. The Albanian diplomatic representative in Vienna said in an interview that following the government's setbacks at Elbasan, Fier, and Betar, and the siege of Valona the Prince's situation was no longer sustainable.

A War Begins: A Short-lived Reign Ends

Sarajevo: The assassination of Archduke Francis Ferdinand and his wife. Cover illustration by Achille Beltrame.

On June 28 1914 the European political picture in which Albanian developments occupied a small corner was dramatically transformed by the assassination of the hereditary Archduke Francis Ferdinand in Sarajevo. This time there was no prospect of averting disaster in Europe with the old formula of conferences at the eleventh hour, treaties, and secret agreements. Within weeks, the "Guns of August" would signal the end of an era in Europe—the era of the Powers.

In Albania the change was slow in making itself felt. The insurrection spread; the uncertainty grew. On June 29, following the disastrous government offensive against the insurgents, Aliotti provided Rome with a pessimistic review of his government's options. "To the extent that we decide to preserve the prince on his throne, Europe must face up to the possibility of failure, or of limited success, that will leave him with only a portion of the coastal area." The other option to consider was that Prince Wilhelm would "demand more European troops to suppress the rebellion, and Austria expresses its willingness to come to his aide, even in the absence of a common action. In that case, the desire to keep the prince in place against the will of the majority of Albanians could draw us into an (Austro-Italian) occupation that it is in (Italy's) interest to avoid at all cost."

Lucius, the German minister, told Aliotti that his advice to Berlin had been that the Prince's position was now untenable since he was opposed by a large majority of the population.[14] He himself had urged the Prince to ask Europe for military support, or to abdicate. Lucius maintained that Prince Wilhelm had made two deeply damaging mistakes. The first had been to dismiss Essad in a manner that was totally unjustified, and without knowing how to replace his influence and his knowledge of the country and its people. The Prince's second mistake was to ignore advice not to neglect the Muslim community in central Albania. In addition, the dispute over Epirus had been the original cause of "the whole tragedy."

Meanwhile, Ismail Kemal returned home professing loyalty to the Prince, and declaring himself optimistic that "with good and diligent government" the crisis could be overcome.

But at a meeting of notables with the Prince in Durrës on July 9, he proposed that the Control Commission assumed control, which would have left the Prince with only nominal power. The Prince firmly rejected Kemal's proposal. Kemal returned to Valona and formed a "committee of public safety" for the province.

Bib Doda, a longtime supporter of the government, acknowledged to Aliotti in a long conversation that the Prince's "aggressive politics towards the Muslims" had been fatal; and Wied was moreover "incapable of taking a decision that would correct the situation and should either ask Europe for the force necessary to impose his will, or abdicate."

Prince Wilhelm's position had become truly desperate. In the aftermath of Archduke Franz Ferdinand's assassination in Sarajevo European politics were increasingly diverted towards the Austro-Serbian crisis and on the threat of world conflict looming slowly but inexorably larger on the horizon. On July 11, the Prince summoned the representatives of the Powers and pleaded with them to live up to their commitments. His support had effectively dwindled to Italy and Austro-Hungary who eyed each other warily in anticipation of the likelihood of being on opposite sides of the coming world conflict. Prince Wilhelm's manner was more pathetic than dramatic as he asked for delivery of the promised loan, the deployment of "international or of Romanian troops," and for new pressure to be applied to Greece to "withdraw its forces from Epirus and force Zographos to withdraw the Greek guerrillas."

In the larger scheme of things Albania was now a minor detail in the widening crisis, though not necessarily so for either Rome or Vienna. The Powers' support was fading and the Prince's appeal was shrugged off, with no action taken. Italy and the Austro-Hungarian Empire were left to deal with a situation that was rapidly deteriorating. The growing tension between the two nations rendered joint action more difficult than ever as each government approached the Albanian situation with the possible consequences to the gathering storm of a world conflict very

Durrës: Ships in the harbor.

much in mind. Italy had little choice but to support the Prince and press for peace negotiations with the insurgents, while at the same time trying to bring about a Greek withdrawal. From Rome's viewpoint the prevailing instability was preferable to armed intervention, or to dividing Albania with Austria into two areas of influence, to cantonization, or worse yet to unilateral intervention by the Austrians. The latter would have required action by Italy, with wider consequences for the European situation.

San Giuliano was careful to reassure the Austrians of Italy's intentions on the one hand, but on the other leaving no doubt that Rome was determined to preserve the prince's throne "to avert the grave danger that could result from his demise."

He seized the occasion to send a clear message to Vienna and Berlin that Italy would react strongly to any attempt to upset the balance in the Adriatic at its expense. His brief to Italy's embassies spells out the situation: "Rome was scrupulous in observing the terms of the Italo-Austrian accord." At the same time, Rome "could not ignore the danger that

Austria, or some other developments, could undermine the agreement and we shall have to protect our interests in the Adriatic." The worst scenario, he goes on, would be "an Albania either partly or entirely under Austrian control." The Italians were also nervous about a possible understanding between Vienna and Athens giving the Greeks a free hand in the south in return for Austrian control of the north.

In mid-July Turkhan Pasha made another swing through the capitals of the Powers to press for the loan but returned empty handed, despite Italian backing and the good will of the other governments involved. Prince Wilhelm got no further with his own request for a strong international force. In the circumstances, the assurances of support from London and Paris had a distinctly hollow ring.

The prince appeared uncertain and "could not decide who should take command of his unruly and multi-ethnic troops" at a moment when leadership and a clear head were sorely needed. In July 28 Albanian insurgents marched on Alessio and Medua. Three days later a group of Albanian leaders landed in (Shengjin or San Giovanni di) Medua from Durrës; and as the situation continued to slide towards disaster, the Serbian population in Kosovo began a series of demonstrations against Austria's tough ultimatum to the Serbian government, delivered three weeks after the assassination of Archduke Franz Ferdinand in Sarajevo.

With an enforced abdication by Wilhelm looming as a distinct possibility the Powers hinted that the prince might first take himself out of harm's way in Europe; and the French and German ministers together with the Russian delegate in Durrës urged their Italian and Austrian counterparts Carlo Alberto Aliotti and Heinrich Löwenthal to convene the Control Commission, including its overseas members, in preparation of eventually taking over control. The commission was to meet the prince and explain the true nature of his situation. King Carol of Romania told Baron Carlo Fasciotti, the Italian minister in Bucharest, on August 2 that even he had advised his nephew to leave Albania "while he could still do so with honor." Rome and Vienna still strove to support the prince's position, but the drums of war– Austria's ultimatum to Belgrade, the mobilizing Powers, the last desperate bids to avoid the conflict–overwhelmed any attempt to settle the Albanian problem through diplomatic efforts.

The international force had begun to unravel. Aliotti noted that the Austrian and German volunteer reinforcements that had arrived in July were slipping away to join their respective regiments. At the same time, Major Kroon, the commander of the gendarmerie, sought a meeting with the Italian minister to report that as more and more of the volunteers left for home the force had effectively ceased to exist and, as a result, it had become impossible to defend the city.

The multi-national naval squadron at Durrës literally sailed away, leaving the Italian ships as the sole representatives of the Powers. Yet Mérey von Kapos-Mére, the Austro-Hungarian ambassador in Italy, hastened to assure - or perhaps warn would be a better word–San Giuliano on August 3 that while strategic considerations had necessitated the withdrawal of the Austrian fleet from Durrës, this did not signal any loss of interest in Albania. Vienna continued to adhere to its agreement with Italy and to the decisions of the London conference.

San Giuliano assured Mérey that Italy had no intention whatever of taking advantage of Austria's temporary withdrawal from the area "to acquire more than equal status." The minister instructed Italian embassies to follow this same line assurance at all times, "so that there will be no doubt of our loyal intentions towards Austria-Hungary." Possibly as a show of continuing unity of purpose the ambassadors of Italy and Austria joined forces in warning the Greek authorities of the dangers menacing Argirocastro.

At the end of July Turkhan Pasha made another trip to Vienna. The funds advanced to the Albanian government by Italy and Austria against the promised, but so far undelivered, international loan were exhausted, and Turkhan was hoping to raise more stopgap financing from the Austrians. But he returned empty-handed, and the Austrians urged him to declare war on Serbia in breach of Albania's neutrality as established in London. A request for funds to Rome also drew a blank.

War had broken out in Europe. Following the departure of the last of the German and Austrian volunteers in early August, the Dutch officers now left for home. The insurgents did not press their advantage and attack the city, but the Catholic montagnard fighters from the north that formed its main garrison went on looting sprees that the gendarmerie was powerless to prevent. Snipers in the hills around Durrës were another hazard for those left in the city, and raids and kidnappings were a nightly occurrence. Following the start of Austrian hostilities against Serbia and the possible implication of Montenegro in the conflict the British government instructed Colonel Phillips to withdraw the British contingent from Alessio and Shkoder. Montenegrins laid siege to the latter city, while inside it fighting broke out between Muslims and Christians.

An Italian and an Austrian colonel took turns to perform the function of governor, and consular officials of the Powers took over the civil administration of the city. On August 13, the Albanian government ran out of money. When the insurgents entered Valona at the end of the month, they were unopposed. The dissolution of the international structure designed to hold the Prince in place was complete. All that was left of the Albanian edifice built by the Powers was the rubble. At Berchtold's suggestion–with San Giuliano's concurrence–the work of the commission appointed to establish Albania's northern borders was suspended.

Prince Wilhelm's reign gave its last tired gasp on September 3. The Prince issued a proclamation in which he affirmed his commitment to and belief in the patriotic movement that was underway, but pointed out that Europe was now in a state of war. He announced that it would be "more useful" if he went to the West for some time, but "though far away would have no other concern but to work for the progress of your noble homeland." He embarked on the Misurata with the princess and his family, leaving the palace in the hands of the International Control Commission headed by the consul Carlo Galli. Wilhelm of Wied made his way to Germany where he re-joined the imperial army and was dispatched to the eastern front.

Treachery, incompetence, an absence of discipline, long standing rivalries and disunity among the beys all contributed to the military disaster in dealing with the insurgency. The ignorance of the Dutch officers about Albania and the Albanians, for example, was lamentable. It is also true that from the start the rebels, backed by neighboring Balkan states (for once united), outnumbered the loyalists by around fifteen thousand men under arms against less than ten thousand. There was no political strategy to sustain the government's military action. The majority of the population had no real understanding of the nature of the confrontation because the leadership had made no attempt to explain it. In laying their plans, the Powers had failed to take the religious factor into

Essad Pasha Toptani shown as head of the government and commander-in-chief following the Prince of Wied's departure.

account and their negligence proved costly in terms of support. Lastly, the lack of leadership was tragically evident as hostility towards the government increased.

Following the Prince's departure, Carlo Durazzo, the Italian head of chancery, supplied a possibly ungenerous and certainly partisan epitaph. The Prince, he wrote to Rome, "had been forced to leave the country hated and despised by many, supported by a few, and mourned by none."

Wilhelm of Wied did not abdicate. He reserved his rights and his claim to the Albanian throne. As far as he was concerned Albania remained his principality *in absentia*. How far this was from reality quickly became apparent.

The insurgents entered the capital and raised the standard of the Sultan. What was left of the Prince's supporters were imprisoned. The remaining members of the Control Commission (Italian, French, and Austro-Hungarian) were informed that their services were no longer required, and left the country. As far as anyone knows, the Commission left without producing the six-monthly report on the new state, as required by the London accord.

Predictably, divisions soon emerged within the insurgency. Militant Muslims pressed for the immediate nomination of an Islamic prince who would also be the religious leader. The Shijak and Kavaja groups chose the Ottoman Prince Burhan Eddin, but Essad Pasha loyalists refused to accept a sovereign. A twenty-five member senate was cobbled together with at its head the Tirana rebel leader Mustapha Ndroqi; and one of its first actions was to send a delegation to Constantinople to offer the Albanian crown to the Sultan asking him to name a prince to rule their country.

Essad Pasha was quicker off the mark, returning to Albania on the heels of Prince Wilhelm's departure at the head of an armed column financed and supplied by the Serbian Prime Minister Nikola Pašić.

On September 20, Essad Pasha moved towards Durrës, which he entered on October 5, installing himself in the Konak (the Turkish term for royal palace). Summoning the head of the provisional government he strong-armed the senate to proclaim him "president of the government of Albania and commander-in-chief." He intended, he said, "to govern until the Albanian people and the Powers chose a new sovereign." He also sent word to the Powers that he had assumed responsibility for the security of foreigners in Albania. If foreigners were reassured, the same couldn't be said of many Albanians. Refugees, both Christian and Muslim poured into Italy, including a number of military personnel still in their uniforms.

Clashes, street disorders, turf wars became frequent, especially in Tirana, as gradually the clock was put back in Albania and the country was carved up into separate enclaves. Essad established control over Durrës and Tirana, the central area. Bib Doda withdrew to Mirdita. The malissori tribes returned to the mountains. The north dissolved into an ancient patchwork of territorial clans, which were no match for an Austrian invasion; Valona became self-governing, and Greece grabbed the south, later to be replaced by Serbia. At about the same time Italy occupied Valona first and gradually the remainder of the territory, with the exception of Korcia, which was held by France.

The Albania envisioned in London had disappeared together with the political arguments and motivations that had brought it into being in the first place. A revival of international interest in the Albanian problem would have to wait until the peace conference following the end of the conflict. For the moment, however, an independent Albania existed, in Giannini's beautiful phrase, as "an ideal, but not a reality."

Italian and Austro-Hungarian Diplomacy in Albania

In both Rome and in Vienna, Albania was seen primarily as the gateway to the Adriatic. The policy that created the complex rivalry between Italy and Austria-Hungary over this particular corner of the Balkans after the Congress of Berlin, was laid down by Tommaso Tittoni, the Italian foreign minister from 1903-1909, and rendered more forceful by the inability of a weakened Ottoman Empire to counter it. "The true value of Albania lies in its harbors and its coastline, the possession of which would give either Italy or Austria-Hungary undisputed supremacy in the Adriatic," Tittoni wrote in 1904. "Italy will never allow Austria-Hungary to achieve this, nor will Austria-Hungary permit Italy. Should one of these two states attempt to gain control over the region, the other would oppose it with all the means at its disposal."

Austria's objective was complete control of the Adriatic, and thus of the Balkan-Danube region, thereby encircling irredentist and pro-Slav Serbia (emerged strengthened from the conflicts in the Balkans) and blocking Serbian access to the sea. Italy feared being bottled up in an Austrian lake. Rome was also jittery about Austro-Hungarian expansionist ambitions in the Orient which would upset the balance of power between the two countries. The strategic key to controlling the Adriatic was the occupation of Mount Lovčen: its twin peaks in southwestern Montenegro just 70 kilometers from Canale d'Otranto, the nearest point in Italy dominate the Bocche di Cattaro (now better known as Boka Kotorska) thus preventing anyone from turning it into a strong naval base—or defending one's own.

74   A Prince Too Far

Bocche di Cattaro seen from Mount Lovčen.

In March 1914 Lovčen surfaced as an issue in sections of the Austrian press that were considered close to the Austro-Hungarian High Command. Editorials urged the government in Vienna not to be squeamish about grabbing the high ground before a widely rumored Serbian alliance with Montenegro gave the Serbs their desired access to the sea. When the newspaper *Militärische Rundschau* reported that the authorities in Vienna would soon take steps to deal with the Lovčen situation, Italian concern became acute.

The Czarist government, forced by its defeat in the war with Japan and by the internal turbulence of the 1905 revolution to stand idly by while Austria-Hungary annexed Bosnia-Herzegovina, had by now reorganized it armed forces and was looking for ways to stage a comeback in Balkan politics. Obsessed with being left out of the loop by the Powers, nervous about Austro-Hungarian intentions, and permanently seeking warm water bases, Russia cultivated a special relationship with Belgrade and supported Serbia's territorial ambitions, but not enough to risk becoming involved in a general conflict.

In a period of widening global tension the Albanian question remained mostly an Italian and Austrian concern. In the final days before the tidal wave of the First World War engulfed all other international issues, the foreign ministers of Italy and Austria, Antonino di San Giuliano and Leopold Berchtold tried to insulate Albanian affairs from the larger and more menacing context. The pair micromanaged the crisis from one day to the next in a manner that is today surprisingly familiar. Some diplomatic operations are not as novel as they are thought to be!

In a sense the Albanians had Italian-Austrian rivalry in the Adriatic to thank for their autonomy and subsequent independence. Chekrezi, the secretary of the Control Commission scornfully labeled the new country "an illegitimate child of Austrian diplomacy with Italy as midwife." Both governments–competitors in other respects– had a shared objective in establishing and supporting a vital and stable Albania, which incidentally its neighbors did not. Nor was it an overriding consideration for the other Powers, except in the interest of stability in the region.

For many years Rome and Vienna had by mutual consent balanced their respective influence in Albania on the basis of "parity." With Italian-Austrian relations becoming more difficult as a result of the worsening situation in Europe both sides tried to prevent their difficulties over Albania from making things worse. The meeting between San Giuliano and Berchtold in Abbazia between April 14 and 18 was an exercise in clearing the air and mutual reassurance. The "parity" in Albania was confirmed, as was their common determination to make every effort to maintain Prince Wilhelm, still wobbly after only a few weeks, firmly in place.

They said they were committed to an "indivisible and independent" Albania and "to the necessity of supporting Wied and to try and prevent his fall." The prince had been in Durrës for a few weeks and already the doctors were fussing around his sick bed.

But the ministers also came up with a prescription for recovery: "1) Advise the Prince to place himself at the head of his troops; 2) promote negotiations for a peaceful settlement between the Albanian government and the Epirotes; 3) hasten the evacuation of Greek forces from territory assigned to the Albanians." The Greeks showed great reluctance to withdraw, particularly after the Italians refused any linkage to the Aegean island issue, and despite Rome's assurances to Venizelos. But while the conflict in southern Albania dragged on Italy and Austria-Hungary faced the equally unwelcome alternatives of losing prestige or coercing the Greeks by force, with the Austrians inclined towards the latter. San Giuliano proposed concessions to the Epirotes, as an alternative pressure on Athens by the Powers, while at the same time building up an effective Albanian military. "Before we threaten force, we need to make sure we can follow through with action," he wrote.

Vienna, obsessed with pan-Slavism, was determined to oppose any move to unify Serbia and Montenegro, which appeared likely with the death of King Nicholas, or even by direct annexation. Berchtold also considered the alternative of enlarging Albania through the addition of areas of both Serbia and Montenegro populated by Albanians.

In a long and detailed letter to King Vittorio Emanuele written in his own hand the foreign minister elaborated on the section of the Abbazia communique–much derided in the Italian parliament–which included a commitment to making "Italian public opinion more sympathetic towards the close relations between Italy and Austria."

The statement had been, he wrote, "the only way to acknowledge the positive discussion that had taken place about the impact of Vienna's treatment of Italians who were Austrian citizens on bilateral relations." In effect, San Giuliano had raised the issue of how Austria treated Italians living under its rule, but he thought it prudent not to make this discussion public so as not to exacerbate already inflamed public opinion. He knew his Austrian interlocutors were aware of "the great influence of this factor on Italian-Austro-Hungarian relations," but, as he confessed to the king, it was part of the problem, not the solution.

Diplomatic relations are not a self-contained universe. In the end, all politics are local, as the saying goes: domestic developments, parliamentary business can be determining factors on how foreign policy issues are decided. The Essad incident and the insurrection crisis underlined the tensions between Austria and Italy over Albania, and provided fresh ammunition for political and media critics in either country about the other. The strategy of the two governments was, on the contrary, to contain the tension and not allow the situation to degenerate, and their bi-lateral relations to suffer, perhaps irreparably. Rome was hoping for progress on the problematic issue of Italian provinces in Austria-Hungary. "The biggest difficulty," San Giuliano complained to the German ambassador in 1914, "is to ensure that the agents of both governments on the ground– both official and unofficial–follow scrupulously the instructions they receive. Unfortunately, that is not always the case either on one side or the other." The reference to "unofficial agents" focuses on the intelligence services of the two powers, both of which were evidently active in Albania. On the basis of what is known, it does not appear that the secret services had different political agendas from that of the government, or at least the respective ministers of foreign affairs. But the military high command to which the agents reported often had views that did not exactly coincide with those of the political ministers. The practice in democracies of placing the armed forces under civilian political control had not yet been firmly established, as the case of Conrad von Hötzendorf[15] in Vienna clearly indicates.

The Muricchio-Chinigò case had deeply embarrassed the respective diplomatic services, but seems not to have triggered the public outcry that it would certainly have caused today. Albania attracted a strange, multi-national collection of "volunteers," most of them career officers, or characters like Biegeleben, a volunteer who ended up as chief of police in Durrës, appointed directly by the Prince. Or like the German adventurer, Baron Gumpelberg who made his last stand commanding a street barrier in Durrës. But they were strange times: the Prince of Sturdza, an attache in the Romanian Legation in Durrës, ended up commanding a battery of Albanian artillery. The campaign to win the hearts and minds of Albanians was delicately referred to in diplomatic correspondence as a "program of moral and cultural affirmation and economic penetration."

Invoking the parity with Austria confirmed at Abbazia, San Giuliano telegraphed Avarna in Vienna to inform Berchtold frankly that, while Austria had more money to spend he (San Giuliano) had always given instructions "to our agents and to so-called Italophiles to make propaganda in favor of Italy, but scrupulously to avoid saying or doing anything that could be construed as anti-Austrian," adding that "Italy's close collaboration with Austria is an absolute necessity for Albania's very existence." The minister was encouraging a non belligerent rivalry. "Both Italy and Austria will continue with their respective propaganda in Albania, but I want Count Berchtold to be persuaded that we have no intention of undermining Austria's influence and even less do we harbor any recondite plans of territorial conquest." The Austrian government focused attention on the Catholics in the area, and both sides sought to influence leading figures in Albanian public life. "It is in our interest to support the Prince of Wied and to consolidate his position," the minister instructed Aliotti in mid-June, with the insurrection at its peak. "But you should

The Marquis of San Giuliano in conversation with Count Berchtold at the conference in Abbazia.

also do everything possible to ensure that the new government will be composed of members favorable to us, without of course showing our hand too much in the process."

In their war of influence Italy and Austria employed every known strategy for boosting their prestige, including all the known propaganda techniques, supported by what for the times was lavish gift-giving. The level of competitiveness would almost have seemed touching, were it not for the fact that the same ploys can be seen in use today on a more sophisticated level, but with much the same purpose in mind.

The press kept careful score of their respective successes. When the Austrians invited three thousand children to the consulate in Shkoder and gave them clothing, the same number of children was hosted at the Italian consulate where they not only received new clothing in the name of Queen Elena of Italy, and were presented with ten *lire* for each family from the king. The Paris newspaper *Le Journal* published a tongue-in-cheek report on the rival efforts to win the hearts and minds of Albanians. The "Italians send two military motor vehicles to transport troops; the Austrians send two military motor vehicles and a staff car for officers. But it was putting the cart before the horse," the paper says, "because the road needed major upgrading to be suitable for automobiles. After lengthy negotiations it was agreed that the road would be divided into three sections: the Austrians modernized the first section, the Italians the second, and the Austrians again tackled the third."

At Durrës the Austrians opened a school where Albanian children were taught free of charge, and given free meals and books. Rome opened its own school, "but needed to offer something extra," *Le Journal* reported, "so the population was informed that at the Italian school, in addition to free schooling, meals, and books, children would receive the sum of two *soldi*. The Italian school now flourishes." The Austrians built a hospital, and the Italians responded by sending a team of two doctors, three assistants, and two nurses, who toured the villages. "The Italians constructed a hotel in Valona," *Le Journal* goes on. "Two weeks after it opened, workers were sent from Vienna. They put up a large shed, which was supposed to be a hotel. It wasn't, but honor was saved."

The propaganda war was continuous in the press. If *Corriere della Sera* reported from Shkoder that, "Italian influence was making great strides," and spoke of improved sea links with Bari and Brindisi, the Viennese paper *Zeit* warned, from the same dateline that Italian trade was surging ahead at Austria's expense; and the *Reich Post* said the Italians had gained in popularity because "they were not active in politics, but concentrated on working with enthusiasm."

Life in Shkoder revolved round the Italian theater and Italian schools, according to the paper. Following the arrival of the Prince of Wied, the *Frankfurter Zeitung* noted Italy's growing commercial influence in Albania. Moreover, "the international language is Italian," the paper stated. As for the Austrian school in Durrës, it was a fifth of the size of the Italian school.

Relations between Italy and Austria on the ground were going from bad to worse, riddled with suspicion on both sides, and not helped by the tension in Durrës itself. In the two capitals, too, the façade of diplomatic entente was beginning to be questioned in Parliament and by the public. In his memoirs, Salandra distances himself from his own minister and stresses that he had little to do with the Albanian question, becoming involved only when he had to, and that "very unwillingly."

On June 22, San Giuliano sent an uncharacteristically candid message to his Austrian counterpart reminding him that, "on one side and the other the freedom of action of both ministers of foreign affairs was limited by internal difficulties." Just as Berchtold faced unexpected obstacles to his foreign policy, such as the Hohenlohe decree, and the actions in Albania of agents probably in the service of other Austrian departments, the Italian government "has to take into account Parliament and public opinion. In this case, it is a constitutional obligation that no government can pursue a course not approved by the majority of the Chamber of Deputies, which has the right to replace that government with another that conforms to its views."

Avarna also delivered to Berchtold another message from San Giuliano, which was at the same time a clarification and a warning. Given a bi-lateral commitment to the agreements in the area of both politics and commerce amounting to the principle of parity, which will form the basis of future instructions, "we must ensure that the accords are applied with parity by both countries. If not, we will be forced to protect our political and commercial interests."

In his reassuring reply, the Austrian minister used almost identical language, Austria-Hungary's political and commercial activity was similarly based on agreements reached with Italy, "which in essence amount to a principle of parity." He denied that "individuals indirectly dependent on the government in Vienna and operating in Albania in the Austro-Hungarian sphere of influence" were responsible for anti-Italian propaganda. He went on to point out that when demonstrations were organized against Italy in Shkoder both the consul and Bishop Sereggi (who was thus confirmed as an Austrian agent) "took steps both on their own initiative and following instructions to put a stop to them."

The climate of growing malaise affected relations between the diplomatic representatives in Durrës, and efforts by the two foreign ministers to persuade them to collaborate produced little improvement. On May 27, San Giuliano sent a telegram to Aliotti urging him to patch up some contretemps with his Austrian counterpart. "I desire that the dispute between Löwenthal and yourself should end immediately, and I rely on your prudence and tact," San Giuliano ordered. And while he was at it, the minister went on, would he instruct the consul in Valona "that it is in our interest that he should do the same, instead of fomenting dissent between Italian and Austro-Hungarian officials in Albania."

In the weeks that followed relations between Italians and Austrians in Durrës and elsewhere in Albania did not improve. When Berchtold accused Aliotti of "conduct that was not always impartial," San Giuliano came to his defense saying that "there was no concrete fact to support this charge against our representative, whereas Löwenthal clearly had exercised personal pressure on Mufid to resign," as the minister of justice, and Libohova, as the minister of religious affairs. The Austrian foreign minister agreed that the two countries should not interfere in Albania's internal affairs, and told Avarna he was eager to see the incident closed. Yet on June 14, San Giuliano sent Aliotti another stern call to order which was in the nature of a personal warning. "In the present international situation good relations between Italy and Austria-Hungary are a major consideration, and an essential dimension of that relationship is that the parity between Italy and Austria regarding Albania remains a reality on the ground, and not fictitious. Therefore our interests and prestige must be managed with loyalty and firmness."

The minister deplored that in May the impression spread that Italy had identified its interests with Essad, which was "harmful (because) it resulted in the more or less open hostility of the Prince, the Dutch, and a large part of the Albanian population, and in disapproval from important Italian and Austrian quarters. I am not passing judgment on your actions, and I well appreciate the difficulties of working in that environment," the minister continued. "I have the impression that at one point you became convinced that the Prince of Wied was destined to fall, and that assessment had conditioned your actions. I do not rule out that events may prove you right, but for the moment is seems that the Prince must stay, and our influence can never match that of Austria if we cannot gain the Prince's favor. If my impression is wrong please explain how I should change it."

Parity was a crucial element in a policy that was linear, but hard to sustain in practice. "We don't have to be submissive. But we must avoid giving Austria the pretext to say that we do not keep our agreements, and provide those who are against us with an opportunity to convince their government to take advantage of Italy's current internal difficulties to undertake some aggressive move in Albania." He concluded by explaining that in such turbulent times in Italy it was important to avoid being forced to send troops out of the country, "even in very small amounts." It was therefore even important to find a solution to the Epirus situation.

Prince Wilhelm's disastrous defeat in Durrës followed a few days later, and a vindicated Aliotti could not resist crowing to his minister. "As for me," he wrote. "I recall the views transmitted in your telegram 3848." That was, of course, the text quoted above.

San Giuliano lost his patience and distributed to all interested embassies a rap on the knuckles directed at Aliotti. "The government's directives are based on a comprehensive vision of our country's interests, taking into account not only Albania, but other situations as well. They take into account the international situation which cannot be totally understood from your perspective. It is absolutely necessary to maintain and even improve the present good relations between the governments of Italy and Austria-Hungary. The respective representatives in Albania must be totally aware that if these relations are compromised no partial recovery in Albania can compensate for the damage and the turbulence to the two Powers and to the whole situation in Europe."

Turning to the specific case involving Aliotti he faulted the minister for pursuing, to the embarrassment of the Rome government, a personal policy that was totally his own based on his personal convictions. San Giuliano had previously defended the integrity of Italy's diplomatic representative in Durrës to Berchtold and to the Germans, but in reality he mistrusted him and considered him dangerous. He even said so to Salandra, who recorded it in his memoirs. "Whereas it was not Austrian officials who undermined Italy's influence, it was you who advised Bib Doda not to aid the Prince. That act was contrary to our commitment to the Prince, to Austria, to Romania, to the Great Powers, and to the general direction of our policy."

San Giuliano portrayed Italy's loss of influence with the Prince of Wied as Aliotti's responsibility. The Prince, the minister wrote, remains in power, "thanks to the support of Albanian Catholics loyal to Austria after he had been put in danger by Muslims, presumed to have been encouraged by Italy." San Giuliano then imposed limitations on his diplomat's freedom of action and summoned him to Rome to discuss with him and the Secretary General "ways to recover (our) lost influence and to put the policy of parity into practice." Later, on August 3, as a follow-up to his first communication, he threatened the consuls in Albania with "immediate recall" if they did not follow rigorously their instructions from Rome.

Aliotti put up a vigorous defense denying that he had advised Bib Doda, claiming that his actions had been farsighted, and pointing out Austrian attempts to undermine him. But San Giuliano's relations with Aliotti had been scarred by mistrust for some time. Following the clashes in Durrës, he let Vienna know that, "as I don't approve some of Aliotti's actions, and believe me if Wied remains it will be in our interest to replace Aliotti," but he would not have been able to carry out his intention, "unless Parliament and the country were convinced of the wisdom of this change."

He would willingly have recalled Aliotti, he would later tell Salandra, "if it were not for the obstacle of public opinion, whose short-lived sentiments about foreign policy should be given less importance that they are in Italy, especially during times of crisis." Aliotti was liked by the Italian press and, it seems, exploited his popularity to gain support for his patriotic views, which had popular appeal. The prime minister recalled in his memoirs that Aliotti was "a quick witted and energetic diplomat," who, however, had a tendency towards over-emphasis. Still, at that moment, "we could have contained him, rather than reject him."

There is no doubt that the apparent contradiction inherent in a complex and acrobatic policy, plus the internal constraints, and the local deprivations that sparked local flashes of unrest demanded constant vigilance on the part of Rome and Vienna. Never has a minister of foreign affairs had to expend so much time and energy on sermons and remonstrations to his diplomatic representatives. One can find fault with the lack of adherence to both the spirit and the letter of instructions; on the other hand, the tense atmosphere of the eve of the world war should be taken into account, together with a certain hostility towards Austria in Italy, and the same in reverse, in equal measure. Even so, officials in a cold and rational profession were not immune from the prevailing crusading spirit.

It is easier to strive to win than to hold one's opponent to a draw, particularly over a long period. Berchtold and San Giuliano were engaged in the latter effort, but they were surrounded by people and forces often favoring the other objective. In Albania, Austrians and Italians suspected each other of plots that were often trivial in nature, and their local psychological warfare in the end damaged both countries. Worse was the impact on their common objective, namely, the emergence of a vital Albania, the only way to ward off, at least temporarily and confined to the Adriatic and the Balkans, the conflict inherent in the Triple Alliance.

Conclusions

The situation in the Balkans today is profoundly changed but also disturbingly similar. The western European powers have coalesced into the European Union, which doesn't make them one entity but provides more room for unified action. Russia and Turkey, radically changed in many respects, still cling to some of their old aspirations. In addition, America has emerged as the world superpower, and as a European power with a role in the Balkans. Even Japan and China have elbowed their way assertively into Balkan affairs. The Atlantic Alliance has emerged as the stabilizing factor collaborating somewhat diffidently with a Russian presence.

On the other hand, while the Balkan protagonists are not those of the past, most of the region's problems have carried over from the early part of the century as a continued source of concern, not to mention a frustrating and bitter *déjà vu*.

The "clash of civilizations" that characterized the century throughout the two world conflicts and the subsequent Cold War years allowed authoritarian and totalitarian regimes to consolidate their grip on the region, and it took one match to rekindle the old flames of nationalism that had ended the Ottoman Empire.

What was most striking was that a sadly familiar scenario was being repeated in the Balkans after barely a century; a scenario dominated once again by ethnic and religious hostility, driven by a repressive form of nationalism and orchestrated by leaders culturally a long way in their perception of the state from the Europe to which they claim to belong.

With the events in Albania in 1914 in mind, it is hard not to make the mental jump to the more recent narrative of Yugoslavia's strife ridden fragmentation, asking the question whether humanitarian considerations require that states founded on religion or nationalism should be supported, and even defended, despite violence carried out in the name of one or the other. In other words, does not such support amount to legitimizing ethnic cleansing? We accepted the post-war ethnic cleansing of Germans from their homes in Central Europe in 1945, possibly to remove a historic element of instability from the region, and also because some degree of vengeful violence against the defeated Germans for horrors committed in the war in the east, and for the Holocaust, was inevitable, and perhaps justified. The peaceful cohabitation of people of different religions and ethnicity is an integral part of our culture protected by human rights. But what about when such cohabitation is clearly impossible, and the cause of violence?

Should we stand by and watch more or less cohesive regions fragment into small and perhaps not viable states, or use superior military and economic pressure to force populations into abstractly conceived political and institutional systems hoping they will take root, and perhaps develop a higher level of conscience?

Stability, both internal and regional, is perceived as primary objectives in helping change. It's hard to consider an intellectual approach while the situation remains inflammatory, but some reflection would seem both necessary and helpful. The problem facing the moral imperatives of the international community is to determine its realistic options in attempting to reduce suffering and injustice. An ideal design is not necessarily a plan of action; but it should form the pragmatic basis of a concrete approach to the situation. The hard choice in foreign policy is always between Bismarckian *Realpolitik* and a Wilsonian moral crusade, order and justice. The dilemma is between systemic stability and revisionism.

The politics of national interest and the power of the state, Ranke's politics, found their fullest expression in the Congress of Berlin, rooted in power, the balance of forces, the secret agreements between governments, and between high commands. They were challenged by the ideas inspired by the French Revolution, elaborated in the liberalism of 1848, with its emphasis on public opinion, open diplomacy, the role of parliament, and respect of civil rights.

The two categories– national interest and moral values– are a bad combination that creates instability. Only very recently have we come to regard moral values (which are different from moralism) as "invisible national interests," as the writer Joseph Nye has called them: elements of the soft power of the Great Powers - the use of culture and economics that can, indirectly and in its own manner, be as effective on the international plane as politico-military hard power.

Once again after less than a century the Great Powers, shocked by human rights violations and angered by another ethnic cleansing, have intervened militarily to put an end to the horror in an unstable region plagued by nationalism, and barbaric hatred and tormented by the atrocities of civil conflict in what was described as "the first humanitarian war."

It's hardly reassuring to witness in our age of globalization a replication of events as they unfolded in 1914, a period of nationalism, pan-Slavism, and at the same time the beginning of the end of the imperial world of the 19th century. To what extent (if at all) is it possible to shape a people and a territory located in an area of instability into a new country? The question was not one raised by the Great Powers to any great extent; possibly because the countries cast loose earlier by the Ottoman appeared to be stable, and not yet troubled by the after-effects of the colonial experience. Thus the debate on which direction to follow was limited to direct versus indirect rule.

The unresolved question, which I believe to be irresolvable in the abstract, one that comes with the necessity to intervene in a foreign country or a foreign territory, includes the problem of having to deal closely with its government, its people, and its elites, however quarrelsome, violent, and untrustworthy they may be.

Once hostilities have been stopped, every such intervention moves on to institution building, the creation of social structures, more modern certainly and more advanced, but alien to the centuries-old existing order. In fact, I do not believe that if the Wied government had brought along a team of sociologists and constitutionalists it would have required to develop the Statute of Valona into a real judicial system, into a state.

We should perhaps ask ourselves whether in 1914 the Powers and the Prince of Wied could have done better, or whether Monsignor Fan Noli had been right in arguing that one could not censure the prince for not being able to perform miracles. But could the Powers have done so? What is the message of the turbulent six-month reign for our times?

The new leadership introduced by the European powers hoped to create a national pride in Albania and a sense of loyalty, but also a certain degree of reverential awe. The naval presence from the world's most powerful states, the guns, the gendarmerie, the international trappings surrounding the new leadership were directed at sending a strong message of encouragement to a small nation emerging from centuries of dominance by the unraveling Ottoman empire that it had the protection of the Powers in the name of Europe and civilization.

It's often easier to initiate military action than it is to establish civil and political institutions, and so the latter effort tends to become secondary; and the same can be said of creating regional stability between the new state and less stable neighbors. Europe's involvement in Albania started well. The local chiefs' acceptance of the Prince on his arrival showed a promise of respect for, and faith in the Powers' choice. Opposition from the political leadership undermined that positive reaction, which faded too quickly, and with it Europe's power to influence developments in Albania.

What remained was alienation from the new sovereign, the gendarmerie, and the foreign ways of the newcomers. The new European formula was a graft that failed to take on the surface of Albanian tribalism and what was left of the Ottoman system. More so since the Albanians had succeeded in gaining their own autonomy and independence, and looked upon the Albania envisioned by the Powers in London as a step backwards from their own earlier achievements.

And indeed, the Albania created by the Powers was the result of territorial compromises and map redrawing (at the expense of neighboring populations) in an effort to balance the forces of the region. In large measure the compromises have endured to present times and remain among the root causes of today's conflicts in the region.

Albania's security was guaranteed by the European Powers, and particularly Italy and Austria who were committed to protect the country's integrity from its rapacious neighbors, from the Serbs, the Montenegrins, the Greeks. Law and order were to have been the responsibility of the gendarmerie formed, trained and officered by the Dutch who, within the limitations of their equipment, showed great commitment. Here again, however, there were problems, including lack of understanding of the country and difficulties in the chain of command, and above all confusion between the typical role of the gendarmerie and that of the armed forces who were supposed to keep the armed insurgents in check. In the end the orders, often at cross purposes, of multi-national troops, sailors performing shore duties, foreign volunteers, adventurers and secret agents of every kind, Albanians with divided loyalties did little more than create chaos and uncertainty, with only marginal control over the country.

Even more uncertain were the institutional foundations of the Prince's power, and therefore the legitimacy of his rule. Who had the authority, and over whom? The Prince had his own view of his role, but he was neither an energetic nor a charismatic sovereign. The Albanian government, set up initially as a gathering of the country's chiefs, was quickly and easily ignored by the Powers and by those with the strongest voice. Essad was no role model. He may have been a conspirator and a triple agent. But his treatment would have dissuaded any Albanian leader from remaining loyal to the government. So the beys remained ensconced in their own lands ready to intervene militarily if eventually after substantial subsidies, and adjusting their loyalties to the prevailing political winds.

Religion contributed to the damage. The mistakes by the prince and the Powers and the intrigues of the clergy of the various denominations turned an atmosphere of tolerance into one of religious fanaticism.

Surprisingly limited personnel and finances were made available for this complex and important political design. With the exception of the naval units which, however, operated independently, the prince was allotted few men and military hardware, and a limited budget. A clause in the London document proposed that he should tap into "the country's resources" to supplement his requirements, but in the circumstances that proved difficult.

The prince never had the time to put in place properly functioning fiscal, financial and judicial mechanisms. In this regard, one obvious factor was the failure of the National Bank of Albania; but also lacking were the energy and innovative vision in addressing the government's other essential functions that might have won over the support of the Albanians. The Wied administration seemed incapable of impressing the population that it could govern better than the old regime and the Ottomans.

What was needed was territorial control, a clear sense of purpose, charisma and authority, sufficient means available, the creation of modern, representational institutions, and also authority to govern free from the external pressure of the Powers. But jealousy and jostling for influence undermined the coordination between Italy and Austria-Hungary, not to mention the intrigues of the other Powers which had sent "agents of influence" towards the Albanian government, raising the question whether this reflects a fundamental flaw in the multinational narrative.

In the Albanian case, the prince took an oath that the well-being of his subjects would be his paramount concern, but for the foreign officers and functionaries their respective countries' interests came first. Some progress has since been made: international and supranational organizations are charged with appointing officials removed from the interests of the country or parties with which they are involved as well as those of their own country. Still, it's hard not to be skeptical when confronted with the no-holds-barred jockeying to secure positions and roles in international organizations.

In reality, the prince's authority and that of his government were undermined from the start by the relationship– or lack of it– between the Powers. "Europe" seemed not to have a clear, coherent political design for Albania which their chosen leader could execute. Apart from Italian and Austrian intentions, the Germans remained neutral, the British distant, and the French and the Russians backed the interests of their respective clients.

Europe's failure to speak with one voice on Albania or to be capable of unified action was exploited by the Ottoman government, with Constantinople playing off the Powers and their clients against each other as the Turks had done for generations to their advantage. The result was a loss of prestige and high moral standards, and a failure to inspire confidence in the Albanians that was fatal to the experiment.

But that Europe was living on borrowed time. The World War would soon bring about its end. The final curtain on the Prince of Wied's reign was rung six months later in the Doomsday that hurtled across Europe trampling failures and successes in its path, the Powers' good intentions and their intrigues–and no one can say it could have ended otherwise.

But it does exempt the Powers of that era from Friedrich Schiller's severe pronouncement: *Weltgeschichte ist Weltgericht*–World history is the world's tribunal.

Notes

1 *Childe Harold's Pilgrimage,* Canto II, stanza XLV: Fierce are Albania's children, yet they lack virtue, were those virtues more mature.
2 Young Turks: Originally a reformist party, but once in power shifted to a nationalist policy which led to the disintegration of the Ottoman Empire.
3 In addition to the *vilayet* of Ioánina and Shkoder, the new map included the *sanjaks* (districts) of Prizren, Novi Bazar, Priština, and Peć, and the *kaza* (administrative division) of Kalkandelen in the *vilayet* of Kosovo, plus the *sanjaks* of Korcia, Ekbasan and Diber in the *vilayet* of Monastir.
4 Austria-Hungary, France, Italy, the United Kingdom, and Russia.
5 Wilhelm of Wied was born March 26, 1876, the third son of Prince Wilhelm of Wied and Princess Marie of the Netherlands, and grandson of the queen of Romania, the writer Elizabeth of Wied, who used the pseudonym Carmen Sylva. Kaiser Wilhelm I was his great-uncle, and he was thus a cousin of Wilhelm II. He married Princess Sophie of Schönburg-Waldenburg and had two children, Maria Eleonora and Carol Viktor, heir to the throne. In the narrative, the Albanian sovereign is referred to as the Prince of Wied, his original title, and it remained his title in Durrës given that at the London conference Albania was designated a principality.
6 Essad Pasha Toptani (Tirana - 1863 - Paris 1908): Turkish officer sent to Albania in 1908. He was minister of the interior in the provisional government, but then formed a second, rival government in Tirana in an unsuccessful attempt to assume control of the country. At the start of the Prince of Wied's reign he was appointed minister of war. Suspected of plotting against the prince he barricaded himself in his house in Durrës, which came under artillery shelling. Banished to Italy, he declared himself regent at the start of World War I and returned to fight the Austrian-Hungarians. With the close of hostilities he tried unsuccessfully to get himself crowned king. He was assassinated in Paris by an Albanian nationalist.

7 The Dutch Major (later Colonel) Thomson was named commander of the Durrës gendarmerie following the dismissal of his fellow countryman Major Sluys for the shelling of Essad Pasha's house. Thomson fell on January 15, 1914, fighting the Muslim insurgents. The following day, his body, wrapped in a white sheet and lying on a stretcher was carried shoulder high through the streets of Durrës.
8 In some Balkan countries *konak* is synonymous with royal palace. The one in Durrës was a hastily converted old Turkish barracks on the seafront.
9 Capt. Castoldi and Baron Buchberger were what amounted to the Italian and Austrian liaison officers respectively at the konak. The contemporary press described them as "court advisers," which did not save them from dismissal during the May uprising.
10 The armed yacht Misurata, formerly Turkish but acquired by Italy in the Libyan War, played an important role in the short-lived reign of Wilhelm of Wied. The Italian vessel was anchored in the bay of Durrës and had multiple functions. It housed officials when accommodation was not available ashore; but it was also where the princess relaxed and even held musical soirees, and where the royal couple sought refuge in June during the uprising.
11 Thomson was very popular with Albanian Muslims; he was in the region between 1905 and 1908 organizing the Ottoman gendarmerie and was sent to Prizren in 1913 to oversee the Serbian retreat.
12 Thomson's funeral was attended by the Prince of Wied, the members of the International Control Commission, diplomats and military commanders. Thomson's successor was another Dutch officer, Maj. Kroon.
13 The notorious Bishop Caciorri supported Austria's Balkan policy, his involvement in the disturbances in Durrës remains far from clear.
14 Lucius was reprimanded by the minister of foreign affairs, von Jagow, for advising the prince without ministerial instructions.
15 Hötzendorf, Franz-Conrad von, Austrian chief-of-staff, supporter of the preventive war, especially against Italy.

Bibliography

The author consulted *Documenti Diplomatici Italiani* (Series Four, vol. XIII and Series Five, vol. I) covering the periods June 28 – August 2, 1914 and August 2 – October 16, 1914 respectively, and was able to consult as-yet unpublished Italian diplomatic documents from the period immediately prior to the above, for which thanks are due to Prof. Pietro Pastorelli, President of the Commission for the Publication of Diplomatic documents.

Biagini, A, *Storia dell'Albania dalle origini ai giorni nostri*, Milan 1998
Chekrezi, C.A., *Albania Past and Present*, New York, 1919
Duce, A., *L'Albania nei rapport italo-austriaci 1897-1913*, Milan 1983
Falaschi. R and Ismail Bey Vlora, *Il pensiero e l'opera attraverso i documenti italiani*, Rome 1985
Giannini, A., *La Formazione dell'Albania*, Rome 1925
Helmreich, E.C., *The Diplomacy of the Balkan Wars,1912-1913*,New York 1938
Pastorelli, P., *L'Albania nella politica estera italiana 1914-1920*, Naples 1970
Puto, Arben, *L'independence albanaise et la diplomatie des grandes puissances 1912-1914*, Tirana 1982
Salandra, A., *La neutralitá italiana*, Milan 1928
San Giuliano, A. di, *Lettere d'Albania*,Rome 1903
Skendi, S., *The Albanian National Awakening*, Princeton 1967
S.M.E., Stato Maggiore Esercito Italiano, *Le truppe italiane in Albania*, Rome 1978
Swire, J., *Albania – The Rise of a Kingdom*, London 1929
Vlora, I.K., *Memoirs*, (English translation by S.Story, London 1920; Italian translation by N.V.Falaschi and R.Falaschi, Rome 1992)

Glossary

Abdul Mejid, Ottoman prince, one of the candidates for the Albanian throne.
Akif (Aqif) Pasha Elbasani, appointed Albanian minister of interior and of war after Essad Pasha Toptani was exiled.
Aliotti, Baron Carlo Alberto, Italian minister at Durrës.
Arbereshe, Albanian colony established in southern Italy and Sicily between the 15th and 18th centuries.
Armstrong, D.Eaton, British officer and private secretary to the Prince of Wied. Author of *The Six Months Kingdom* (a diary), (Tirana: Albanian Institute for International Relations, 2001).
Avarna, Giuseppe, Duke of Gualtieri, Italian ambassador in Vienna.
Bekir Aga bey (Beqir Grebene), Albanian conspirator linked to the Young Turks, sentenced to death following the failed coup d'état of February 1914.
Berchtold, Leopold Graf, Austro-Hungarian foreign minister.
Besa, ancient oath of peace or truce by which Albanian clan chiefs could suspend hostilities.
Bib Doda (Preng Pasha) "prince" of the Mirdita tribe.
Biegeleben, Freiherr Ludwig von, (nephew of Baron Maximilian von Biegeleben, minister plenipotentiary in the Austro-Hungarian ministry of foreign affairs), Austrian volunteer in Albania, appointed by the prince controller of the Albanian police.
Boletini Isa, leader of the Kosovar insurgents against the Turks.
Bollati, Riccardo, Italian ambassador in Berlin.
Buchberger, Karl von, court adviser to the prince.
Burghele, E, Romanian minister in Albania, dean of the diplomatic corps in Durrës.
Burhan Eddin, Ottoman prince, son of Sultan Abdul Hamid II, possible candidate for the Albanian throne.
Caciorri (Kacori), Monsignor Nicol, Roman Catholic bishop and vice-president in the first Albanian provisional government.
Carmen Sylva, literary pseudonym of writer and poet Elisabeth of Wied, queen of Romania and aunt of the Prince of Wied.
Castoldi, Fortunato, captain in the army unit for diplomatic missions attached to the Italian foreign ministry and adviser to the prince.

Glossary 99

Conrad von Hötzendorf, Freiherr Franz, field-marshal, Austro-Hungarian chief of-general-staff.
De Weer, W.J.H., general, commander of the Albanian gendarmerie, a Dutchman as were Major Sluys, Col. Thomson, and Major Kroon, all of whom succeeded the general.
Djurasković, Vuk, transplanted Montenegrin, mayor of Durrës and Essad Pasha's secretary.
Durazzo, Marquis Carlo, Head of Cancery of the Italian Legation in Durrës.
Essad, Pasha Toptani, president of the senate in the first Albanian provisional government, subsequently Albanian minister of war and interior minister, and then head of the government following the departure of the Prince of Wied.
Fasciotti, Baron Carlo, Italian minister in Bucharest.
Flotow, Hans von, German ambassador in Rome.
Galli, Carlo, Italian consul in Shkoder and a member of the International Control Commission.
Gheghi, Albanian term for a group of dialects spoken by the *gege,* northern Albanians inhabiting the country north of the Shkumbin River.
Grey, Sir Edward, British foreign secretary.
Imperiali di Francavilla, Marquis Guglielmo, Italian ambassador in London.
Ismail Kemal bey Vlora, Albanian patriot, head of the first provisional government.
Izzet (Izet) Pasha, Turkish field marshal and minister of war.
Jagow, Gottlieb von, German minister of foreign affairs.
Kaza', an administrative territory in the Ottoman Empire administered by a *kaimakan.*
Kraal, August Ritter von, Austrian member of the International Control Commission.
Kanun, The so called Lek law is an ancient codification of Albanian traditions and customs.
Löewenthal von Linau, Heinrich, Austro-Hungarian minister in Durrës.
Lucius von Stödten, Helmuth, German minister in Durrës.
Malissori, (mountain people), the term used to identify the clans living in Malissia, the mountainous region in northern Albania.
Mbret, Albanian form of address to a reigning sovereign or prince.
Mérey von Kapos-Mére, Kaietan, Austro-Hungarian ambassador in Rome.
Mirditi, Roman Catholic tribes in the mountains of northern Albania, mainly centered on the city of Lezhe. Under Ottoman rule they enjoyed considerable autonomy, with their own prince.
Mufid (Myfid) bey Libohova, Albanian minister of justice and religious affairs.

Mufti, Arabic term for Muslim cleric or an individual authorized to interpret the law.

Muricchio, Vincenzo, Italian Army colonel, instructor with the Ottoman gendarmerie (1905-1908), and later (1913) sent to Prizren by the Italian government to oversee implementation of the decisions of the London Conference.

Musa Qasim, *mufti* of Tirana.

Mustafa Ndroqi, president of the Albanian Senate in the Durrës government formed following the departure of the Prince of Wied.

Noli, Monsignor Fan (Theophanes) Stylian, Orthodox cleric, founder of an Albanian church in America, translator of Shakespeare and Ibsen, at the end of the World War, headed the Albanian delegation to the Geneva Conference, minister of foreign affairs and later prime minister, deposed by Zog.

Papoulias, Anastasios, Greek general commanding the forces of the Hellenes in "northern Epirus."

Pašić, Nikola, Serbian prime minister and foreign minister.

Pashalik, administrative region of the Ottoman Empire administered by a pasha.

Paternò Castello, Antonino, Marquis of San Giuliano, parliamentarian, senator, Italian foreign minister, former ambassador in London and in Paris.

Paterno' Castello, Maria, Marchioness of Capizzi (née Paterno' di Carcaci), daughter-in-law of the Marquis of San Giuliano. Widowed prematurely, she corresponded with San Giuliano.

Phillips, G.F., Lieut. Col., the West Yorkshire Regt., commander of the International Force at Shkoder.

Sazonov, Sergej Dmitrević, Russian foreign minister.

Sereggi (Serreqi), Monsignor Giacomo, Catholic archbishop of Shkoder.

Sturdza, Prince Mihail, Attaché at the Romanian Legation in Durrës.

Trifari, Eugenio, Rear-Admiral, Italian Navy and commander of Italy's naval squadron at Durrës.

Turkhan, Pasha Permeti, Albanian prime minister, formerly Turkish ambassador in St Petersburg.

Venizelos, Eleuterios Kiriakos, Greek prime minister and minister of the navy, one time minister of war, and of foreign affairs.

Zogu, Ahmed bey (Zogolli Mati), Albanian leader, prime minister following the World War who seized power in 1924, proclaiming himself king of Albania as Zog I.

Zographos, Gheorghios Christakis, former Greek foreign minister, governor of Epirus, and later head of the provisional government of Epirus of the North.

Photo Gallery

The photographs in this book were first published in 1984 in *Diario fotografico del Marchese di San Giuliano* (Photographic Diary of the Marquis of San Giuliano) by Giuseppe Giarrizzo (with essays by Diego Mormorio and Ferdinando Salleo). They are among the 310 postcards sent by the marquis to his daughter-in-law between March and September 1914. Some were commercial postcards, but most were photographed scenes reduced to postcard size of what the marquis called "the events of Durrës." The photographs were found at a flea market in Palermo in the 1960s. Additional illustrations were reproduced from contemporary publications.

1. Italo Sulliotti, special correspondent in Albania of the Italian weekly Tribuna Illustrata photographed on a ship of the Italian Navy holding onto his hat.

2. Sulliotti (center, holding cup) in a crowded café in Durrës with Albanian insurgents.

3. Albanian women folklore dancers in Durrës.

4. Workmen installing iron grills on the windows of the royal palace in Durrës in preparation for the Prince of Wied's arrival.

5. Work on the interior of a bedroom in the royal palace in preparation for the prince's arrival.

6. Durrës street scene.

7. Arrival of the Prince of Wied: A reception committee of senior officers of the European Powers together with the Austro-Hungarian minister in Durrës, Löwenthal (in civilian clothes) being rowed out to the prince's ship.

8. Arrival of the Prince of Wied: Albanians boarding boats in Durrës to welcome the prince.

9. Arrival of the Prince of Wied: The prince and princess (facing camera) being transferred by launch to step ashore for the first time in Durrës accompanied by Essad Pasha Toptani (back to camera).

10. British Army Col. G.F. Phillips, commander of the International Force in Shkoder with local dignitaries.

11. Baron Carlo Alberto Aliotti, the Italian minister in Durrës, awaits the prince's arrival on the steps of the royal palace with officers of the Italian Navy.

12. A military band playing outside the Italian Legation in Durrës.

13. Top hatted leaders of the Italo-Albanian community outside the Italian Legation.

14. Durrës: Crowds gather outside the royal palace.

15. Durrës: Essad Pasha Toptani (center in uniform) with Albanian dignitaries.

16. Dutch officers inspects Albanian cavalry in Durrës.

17. The Prince and Princess of Wied out riding in Durrës with members of the court and escort.

18. The Prince and Princess out with their two children, Maria Eleonora and Carl Viktor.

19. The Prince and Princess (with parasol) of Wied and their daughter.

20. Durrës: The infant Carl Viktor in the arms of his nurse.

21. Durrës: The princess's ladies-in-waiting outside the royal palace.

22. The Princess of Wied.

23. Princess and daughter visit infant school in a poor quarter of the city. Group includes lady-in-waiting, and member of the palace guard in traditional uniform.

24. Politicians address a crowd in Durrës.

25. Public demonstration in support of the prince in Durrës.

26. Street scene during days of tension in Durrës.

27. Armed irregulars outside the royal palace in Durrës.

28. Albanian soldiers aided by civilians haul an artillery piece and limber in Durrës.

29. Albanian troops and irregulars taking their ease at a gun position on the outskirts of Durrës.

30. Insurgents on the move outside Shijak.

31. Malissori fighters outside the royal palace refusing to fight the insurgents.

32, Italian sailors mounting guard at the royal palace in Durrës.

33. The Austro-Hungarian minister leaving the royal palace in Durrës trailed by aides.

34. Italian officers hold a street conference near a machine-gun in Durrës.

35. Durrës: Italian sailor on guard duty and friends.

36. Austrian sailors man a barricade in front of their country's legation in Durrës.

37. Bishop Caciorri visiting Italian Navy personnel at a defensive outpost in the provisional Albanian capital.

38. A Nationalist outpost at Durrës.

39. Albanian regulars manning a machine-gun post.

40. Albanian troops man a dugout in the fighting at Durrës.

41. Albanian troops bivouac in the same area.

42. A coastal battery in an old Venetian fort in Durrës.

43. Prince Wilhelm returning to Durrës after inspecting government defences.

44. Christian irregulars photographed with Albanian troops and Austrian, British, and French officers.

45. Fifteen hundred fighters loyal to Preng Bib Doda entering Durrës.

46. May 23 at 15.30, in the face of insurgent advances, the Prince and Princess board an Italian Navy launch to embark on the yacht Misurata.

47. The Austrian Navy transporting Malissori fighters out of Durrës.

48. Muslim refugees quit Durrës.

49. Irregular troops on board a vessel in Durrës Harbor.

50. Members of the International Control Commission hold roadside talks at Sijak with insurgents demanding the overthrow of Prince Wilhelm.

51. Durrës street scene with horse-drawn vehicle probably carrying members of the International Control Commission.

52. Durrës street scene with automobile carrying wounded from the fighting.

53. Durrës street scene with stretcher party of the Austrian Navy carrying wounded fighter.

54. Albanian troops and others near a tent serving as a field mortuary.

55. Fighters preparing coffins behind the lines in Durrës.

56. Victim of street fighting carried to the rear in Durrës.

57. June 16, funeral of the Dutch Col. Thomson.

58. June 16, Prince Wilhelm and other officers and officials in Col. Thomson's funeral cortege.

59. June 16, Prince Wilhelm (center) at the burial of Col. Thomson in Durrës.

60. Livestock market in Shkoder.

61. Shkoder: Albanian troops, Malissori fighters, and European officers pose for group photograph.

62. The bishop of Shkoder celebrates open-air Mass.

63. Girls' school in Shkoder.

64. Students of the Austrian military school Polar Stern in Shkoder.

65. The multi-national military force deployed in Shkoder held parades and social functions such as this ceremony at the St Francis of Sales boarding school presided over by the local bishop.

66. Austrian officers occupy the front row of the St Francis of Sales ceremony.

67. Military school students in Shkoder.

68. A gathering of European military officers in Shkoder.

69. Col. Phillips (right foreground), commander of the multi-national military force in Shkoder heads a group of officers taking the salute at a parade.

70. The French contingent, in colonial uniform, march past.

71. The British contingent and band standing at ease waiting for the order to join the parade.

72. The British military band on the move.

73. Rear view of the French contingent .

74. The Italian military band marching past the reviewing officers.

75. Italian troops of the multi-national force.

76. Col. Phillips inspects Italian troops on parade in Shkoder.

77. A group of European officers in conversation following the parade.

78. European officers and civilians at a garden party in Shkoder.

79. Officers of the multi-national force at a social function in Shkoder.

80. Italian officers and their ladies roller-skating in Shkoder.

www.ingramcontent.com/pod-product-compliance
Lightning Source LLC
Chambersburg PA
CBHW031315150426
43191CB00005B/246